STUDY GUIDE FOR USE W

MW01015737

FIRST CANADIAN EDITION

MARKETING

STUDY GUIDE FOR USE WITH

FIRST CANADIAN EDITION

MARKETING

Berkowitz   Kerin   Rudelius   Crane

PREPARED BY

ERICA S. MICHAELS
FREDERICK G. CRANE
Dalhousie University

IRWIN
Homewood, IL 60430
Boston, MA 02116

Printed in the United States of America.

ISBN 0–256–10229–5

2 3 4 5 6 7 8 9 0 P 8 7 6 5 4 3 2

INTRODUCTION

Dear Student:

This guide is designed to give you, the marketing student, every advantage in mastering the concepts presented in <u>Marketing</u>, 1st Canadian Edition, by Eric N. Berkowitz, Roger A. Kerin, William Rudelius, and Frederick G. Crane. Used as a comparison text, this study guide will provide you with a competitive edge by identifying and organizing the most important terms, concepts, and applications in an interesting, concise, and educationally sound manner. If used properly, the study guide should actually reduce the amount of time needed to study for your exams.

The key to the success of this guide is: USE it. Read your <u>Marketing</u> text chapters once through without stopping to highlight or take notes. Enjoy it and digest the material as you go. Read for the purpose of obtaining an overview. Then use your study guide. Start with the section of terms and definitions. If you cannot remember a particular term or its meaning, return to your text for more in-depth understanding. When you have mastered the terms and definitions, continue working the study guide chapter exercises. The exercises follow the same content divisions as your text. It is at this point that you return to the text to glean the highlights of information that make the difference between the "A" student and other students.

It's worth the price of the study guide to WRITE in it. The terms used in this text are terms used in the real marketplace. Writing the terms out in longhand will reinforce your knowledge of the material as well as provide proper professional writing habits for the future. Finally, check yourself for test readiness by using the Quick Recall section at the end of each chapter. Not only should you be able to list the answers to these questions, but you should also be able to define, describe, and demonstrate these concepts thoroughly. If you cannot, return to that specific section in your text and study guide, and review the material.

Use these techniques for each chapter BEFORE the material is covered in class. This enables you to ask intelligent questions and obtain additional information that you may otherwise have missed. Since this text is often used for large sections of introductory marketing, some students find that not all of their needs can be met in the classroom. For this reason, the study guide has included a number of challenge exercises. These exercises are optional; they represent activities that might occur if class sections were small enough.

After looking through this study guide, you will notice that it differs from other study guides in several ways. 1) There are no true/false or multiple choice questions. This was done intentionally. There is no reason to reinforce incorrect information while a student is still in the process of mastering material. This should not hurt you in terms of performing well on an objective test. Material in this study guide is "learned", not "memorized." You should be equally prepared whether your professor's exams are multiple choice, short answer, or essay. 2) Whenever possible, examples used are drawn from actual marketing problems and solutions. This helps tie in the text material with real life. A higher interest level will reflect itself in more efficient learning. 3) Some questions have numerous possible correct answers. Many students find this aggravating. However, one of the key principles of marketing is that there are often many viable alternatives and few clear cut decisions. These questions make you responsible for thinking and being creative. Don't panic! Page numbers from the text are supplied to provide you with appropriate guidelines.

The simple fact that you have purchased this study guide is an indication that you are concerned with doing your best. Marketing is an exciting and dynamic field. We hope this study guide, when used in conjunction with your text, will provide you with the extra edge needed to be successful. Good luck!

Frederick G. Crane
Erica S. Michaels

CONTENTS

1

MARKETING: A FOCUS ON THE CONSUMER

TERMS AND DEFINITIONS

Listed below are the definitions of important marketing terms. Choose the correct term for each definition from the list below, and write it in the space provided.

Business ethics
Consumerism
Controllable factors
Environmental factors
Exchange
Macromarketing
Market
Marketing
Marketing concept
Marketing concept area
Marketing mix

Marketing program
Micromarketing
Organizational buyers
Production era
Sales era
Societal marketing concept
Target market
Ultimate consumers
Uncontrollable factors
Utility

1. _____ Individuals who use the goods and services purchased for a household.

2. _____ Period of North American business history when firms could produce more than they could sell and the focus was on hiring more salespeople to find new markets and customers.

3. _____ The process of planning and executing the conception, pricing, promotion, and distribution of ideas, goods, and services to create exchanges that satisfy individual and organizational objectives.

4. _____ The marketing mix actions (product, price, promotion, place) a manager can take to solve a marketing problem.

5. _____ The study of the aggregate flow of a nation's goods and services to benefit society.

6. _____ A plan that integrates the marketing mix to provide a product, service, or idea to prospective consumers.

7. _____ Establishments such as manufacturers, retailers, or government agencies that buy for their own use or for resale.

8. _____Current period of North American business history that is consumer oriented so organizations strive to produce products that reflect consumer wants while achieving organizational objectives.

9. _____Value for consumers using the product.

10. _____Forces that are largely beyond the control of the marketing department and its organization.

11. _____The view which holds that an organization should assess and satisfy the needs of its customers while also providing for society's welfare.

12. _____One or more specific groups of potential consumers toward which an organization will direct its marketing program.

13. _____A movement started in the 1960's when consumers sought to obtain a greater say in the quality of the products they buy and the information they receive from sellers to increase their influence, power, and rights when dealing with institutions.

14. _____People with the desire and with the ability to buy a specific product.

15. _____The idea that an organization should seek to satisfy the wants of customers while also trying to achieve the organization's goals.

16. _____The marketing activities of an individual organization.

17. _____A marketing manager's controllable factors, the marketing actions he or she can take in specific circumstances. They are: product, price, promotion, place.

18. _____Period of North American business history when goods were scarce so it was assumed they would sell themselves.

19. _____The trade of things of value between buyer and seller so that each is better off after the trade.

20. _____Guidelines that indicate how to act rightly and justly in a business situation.

MARKETING: A DEFINITION TO FOCUS ON NEEDS

"The focus of marketing is on assessing and satisfying customer needs."

Decide which of the following statements demonstrate assessing needs, and which statements demonstrate satisfying needs.

1. _____ A local newspaper phones its customers to inquire about the quality of their paper delivery.

2. _____ A restaurant designates part of its seating as a "non-smoking" section.

3. _____ A dentist starts office hours at 6:30 a.m. for patients who work "nine to five."

4. _____ A new laundry product comes with the offer of a 50-cents-off coupon upon the completion of a mail-in questionnaire.

5. _____ A diaper manufacturer develops a disposable diaper with resealable tapes.

6. _____ An ice cream parlour has its patrons vote for their favorite ice cream flavour.

7. _____ A locally owned supermarket places a suggestion/request box at the service counter.

8. _____ A company sells a low-calorie, nonstick cooking spray for weight-conscious cooks.

PRODUCTION ERA, SALES ERA, MARKETING CONCEPT ERA

There are three distinct eras North American businesses have gone through. Match the descriptive statements to the correct era.

> Product era
> Sales era
> Marketing concept era

I. A survey shows 3 out of 10 mothers do not make use of an exercise facility because there is no available child care.

1. _____ Too bad. We're the only place in town. If they want to work out, they'll work out here.

2. _____ We should examine the feasibility of opening a room and hiring a baby-sitter.

3. _____ We should direct our advertising more toward single or childless women.

II. Sales of our orange-flavoured soft drink have dropped off drastically in the last 2 months.

1. _____We better do some consumer research to see if we can identify the problem.

2. _____It's just as inexpensive to make the cherry flavour instead; we'll give that a try.

3. _____Hire new sales reps; these guys must be slacking off.

TARGET MARKETS

"Because an organization doesn't have the resources to satisfy the needs of all consumers, it selects a target market - a subset of the entire market on which to focus its marketing program."

I. Listed below are markets and specific products. Can you suggest at least two possible target markets for each product?

Market	Product	Target Market
1. People who travel on airlines	Non-meat meals	a._____ b._____
2. People who stay at hotels	Rooms with computer terminals	a._____ b._____
3. People who buy canned foods	Single-serving soups, stews, etc.	a._____ b._____
4. People who buy floor covering	Thick, white shag carpeting	a._____ b._____

II. Listed below are markets and target markets. Can you suggest possible products (goods or services)?

Market	Target Market	Product
1. People who exercise	Young mothers with small children	a._____ b._____
2. Young adults (18-22)	College students	a._____ b._____
3. Pet owners	People who have pets but who must travel extensively	a._____ b._____

MARKETING MIX - FOUR P's

The four elements of marketing mix include:

1. Product - a good or service to satisfy the consumer's needs
2. Price - the amount paid for the product
3. Promotion - means of communication between buyer and seller
4. Place - a means of getting the product into the consumer's hands

"The marketing mix elements are called 'controllable' factors because they are under the control of the marketing department in an organization."

Identify whether these statements reflect decisions of product, price, promotion, or place. Fill in the blank with the appropriate factor.

Example: <u>promotion</u> - A supermarket offers free samples of a new frozen pizza.

1. _____ A vacuum cleaner company manufactures a new light-weight vacuum cleaner.

2. _____ A shoe repair store places a quarter-page ad in the "Yellow Pages".

3. _____ A manufacturer of children's wear negotiates distribution rights with new retailers in three provinces.

4. _____ An art museum suggests a donation of $2.00 at the door.

5. _____ A car battery comes with a life-time guarantee.

6. _____ A manufacturer of clothespins claims in its 30-second radio spots to keep your clothes "hanging in there."

7. _____ A health maintenance organization charges a set fee for its services.

8. _____ The Victorian Order of Nurses provides care directly within the patient's home.

9. _____ An automobile motor oil comes with a $1.00 rebate.

10._____ A greeting card company markets over three hundred different birthday cards.

11._____ A playing card company prices its deluxe line of playing cards $0.75 higher than its competitors' cards.

12._____ A candy bar company offers one line of its candy bars "without nuts."

13._____ A maker of lingerie decides to use the "party plan" method of selling the product line.

14. _____Tupperware has over 200,000 independent contractor dealers who market its entire product line.

UNCONTROLLABLE, ENVIRONMENTAL FACTORS

"There are a host of factors largely beyond the control of the organization and its marketing department." Factors may be:

> Social
> Technological
> Economic
> Competitive
> Regulatory

What factor would most likely account for each of the following situations?

1. _____Many people refuse to purchase products manufactured in countries that violate human rights.

2. _____The advent of a good, inexpensive disposable razor has had an effect on the "shaving" industry.

3. _____The value of the Canadian dollar on the foreign exchange market is constantly changing.

4. _____In most provinces, legislation requires children under four years of age to be placed in car seats or seat belts.

5. _____Crest lost market share when Colgate came out with toothpaste in a pump dispenser instead of a tube.

CONTROLLABLE AND UNCONTROLLABLE INFLUENCING FACTORS

"Recent thinking and marketing successes have shown that a forward looking, action-oriented firm can often _influence_ even some environmental factors."

Consider the following statements carefully. If the statement reflects a controllable factor, put "P." If the statement reflects an environmental factor, put "E." If a statement is an uncontrollable factor that can possibly be _influenced_, put "I." There may be more than one answer per question.

> P   Controllable, four P's, marketing mix.
> E   Environmental, uncontrollable.
> I   Can possibly be influenced.

1. _____Recently, Canadian legislation has banned cigarette advertising in all media.

2. _____ A local car dealership advertises, "We won't be undersold!"

3. _____ A local School Board banned chocolate milk from the school cafeteria because they claimed it made the children too rambunctious after lunch.

4. _____ To boost sales of their automobiles, Chrysler Canada is offering its buyers a 7 year or 115,000 km. warranty.

5. _____ Stock market hits an all-time high.

6. _____ A family restaurant offers a special "buy one dinner - get one free."

7. _____ Contac C offers free foil-wrapped product samples at local drugstore counters.

8. _____ All economic indicators predict an impending recession.

*Challenge - Explain possible ways you as a marketing manager would help influence the outcome for all answers marked "I."

QUICK RECALL

I.   The twin objectives of marketing are:

1. _____

2. _____

II. In order for marketing to occur, at least four things are required:

1. _____

2. _____

3. _____

4. _____

III. Name three distinct eras North American businesses have gone through.

1. _____

2. _____

3. _____

IV. In our free-enterprise system, which three specific groups benefit from effective marketing?

1. _____

2. _____

3. _____

V. The marketing mix consists of four <u>P</u>'s, or controllable factors. They are:

1. _____

2. _____

3. _____

4. _____

VI. The four utilities created by marketing are:

1. _____

2. _____

3. _____

4. _____

TERMS AND DEFINITIONS

1. ultimate consumer	11. societal marketing concept
2. sales era	12. target market
3. marketing	13. consumerism
4. controllable factors	14. market
5. macromarketing	15. marketing concept
6. marketing program	16. micromarketing
7. organizational buyers	17. marketing mix
8. marketing concept era	18. production era
9. utility	19. exchange
10.uncontrollable factors	20. business ethics

MARKETING: A DEFINITION TO FOCUS ON NEEDS

1. assessing   3. satisfying   5. satisfying   7. assessing
2. satisfying   4. assessing   6. assessing   8. satisfying

PRODUCTION ERA, SALES ERA, MARKETING CONCEPT ERA

I. 1. production   II. 1. marketing
    2. marketing   2. production
    3. sales   3. sales

TARGET MARKETS

There are many possible correct answers. For further guidance refer to your text page(s): 12-14.

I.   TARGET MARKETS

1. vegetarians, dieters, religious groups
2. sales reps, executives, travelers with teenage children
3. senior citizens, singles, students
4. young professional singles, older married couples whose children have left the nest, luxury office suites

II.   PRODUCT OR SERVICE

1. rowing machine for home use, no exercise at all, spa with childcare facilities
2. fast foods, discount magazine subscriptions, typing services
3. pet carriers, pet motels, animal medications for travel sickness

MARKETING MIX - FOUR P'S

1. product	6. promotion	11. price
2. promotion	7. price	12. product
3. place	8. product	13. distribution
4. price	9. price, or promotion	14. place
5. product	10. product	

UNCONTROLLABLE, ENVIRONMENTAL FACTORS

1. social
2. technological
3. economic
4. regulatory
5. competitive

CONTROLLABLE AND UNCONTROLLABLE INFLUENCING FACTORS

1. E, I
2. P
3. E, I
4. P
5. E
6. P
7. P
8. E

QUICK RECALL

I.
1. assessing needs
2. satisfying needs

II.
1. two or more parties with unsatisfied needs
2. a desire and ability to satisfy them
3. a way for the parties to communicate
4. something to exchange

III.
1. production era
2. sales era
3. marketing concept era

IV.
1. consumers who buy
2. organizations that sell
3. society as a whole

V.
1. product
2. price
3. promotion
4. place

VI.
1. form
2. place
3. time
4. possession

2

MARKETING IN THE ORGANIZATION: AN OVERVIEW

Listed below are the definitions of important marketing terms. Choose the correct term for each definition from the list below, and write it in the space provided.

Business firm
Distinctive competency
Diversification
Goal setting
Market development
Market penetration
Market segmentation
Market share
Marketing plan
Marketing strategy
Marketing tactics

Non-profit organization
Organizational business (mission)
Organizational goals
Planning gap
Product cannibalism
Product development
Profit
Situation analysis
Strategic management process
Strategic marketing process

1. _____ The steps taken at the product and market levels to allocate marketing resources to viable marketing positions and programs.

2. _____ The reward to a business firm for the risk it undertakes in offering a product for sale; the amount of revenues in excess of expenses.

3. _____ The difference between the projection of a new goal and the projection of the results of a plan already in place.

4. _____ The process of dividing a large market with diverse needs into submarkets, or segments, of prospective buyers with similar needs.

5. _____ An organization that carries on economic activity to earn a profit.

6. _____ The principal competitive strengths or advantages of an organization in terms of marketing, technological, and financial resources.

7. _____ The ratio of sales revenue of the firm to the total sales revenue of all firms in the industry, including the firm itself.

8. _____A statement about the type of customer an organization wishes to serve, the specific needs of these customers, and the means or technology by which it will serve these needs.

9. _____An organization that carries on economic activity to serve the needs of special segments of the public.

10. _____The detailed day-to-day operational decisions essential to the overall success of marketing strategies.

11. _____The gaining of sales by a new product merely by stealing them from those made by one of the company's other products.

12. _____Actions characterized by a specified target and a marketing program to reach it.

13. _____The specific objectives an organization seeks to achieve and by which it can measure its performance.

14. _____The steps taken at the organization's corporate and divisional levels to develop long-run master strategies for survival and growth.

15. _____Taking stock of where the firm or product has been recently, where it is now, and where it is likely to end up using present plans.

16. _____Setting measurable marketing objectives to be achieved.

17. _____A written statement that identifies the target market; specific marketing goals such as units sold, sales revenue, and profit; and the budget and timing for the marketing mix elements that make up the marketing program.

18. _____A strategy of changing the product itself but selling it to existing markets.

19. _____A strategy of developing new products and selling them in new markets.

20. _____A strategy of selling existing products to new target markets.

21. _____A strategy of increasing sales of present products in their existing markets.

BUSINESS (MISSION)

"An organization's business, or mission, is a statement about the type of customer it wishes to serve, the specific needs of the customers, and the means or technology by which it will serve these needs."

The "mission" can dramatically narrow or broaden the range of marketing opportunities available.

For each of the companies selling these products or services, give at least three possible "business" or "mission" statements.

A. Bicycles   1._____

                    2._____

                    3._____

B. Herbal Tea   1._____

                    2._____

                    3._____

C. Hair Salon   1._____

                    2._____

                    3._____

ORGANIZATIONAL GOALS

"An organization must translate the broad statement of its business, or mission, into its organizational goals, specific goals it seeks to achieve to use in measuring its performance."

Several different objectives have been identified that business firms can pursue, each of which has some limitations. Match the organizational goals with the correct definition.

Market share
Profit
Sales revenue
Social responsibility
Survival
Unit sales

1. _____ A firm may choose to increase or maintain its market share sometimes at the expense of greater profits if industry status or prestige is at stake.

2. _____ Respond to advocates of corporate responsibility and seek to balance conflicting goals of consumers, employees, and stockholders to promote overall welfare of all these groups, even at the expense of profits.

3. _____ Achieve as high a financial return on its investment as possible.

4. _____ Choose a safe action with reasonable payoff instead of one with a large return that may endanger the company's future.

5. _____ If profits are acceptable, a firm may elect to maintain or increase its sales level even though profitability may not be maximum.

6. _____ Sales revenue may be very deceiving because of the effects of inflation so a firm may choose to maintain or increase the number of units it sells.

*Challenge - Using Figure 2-3 in the text as a guide, write both the business statement and organizational goals you might use if you were the president of a company manufacturing garden tools.

NON-PROFIT ORGANIZATIONAL GOALS

The organizational goals of a non-profit organization differ somewhat from other business firms. However, their objectives are just as important.

List five possible organizational goals you might have if you were the head of United Way.

1. _____

2. _____

3. _____

4. _____

5. _____

STRATEGIC MARKETING PROCESS

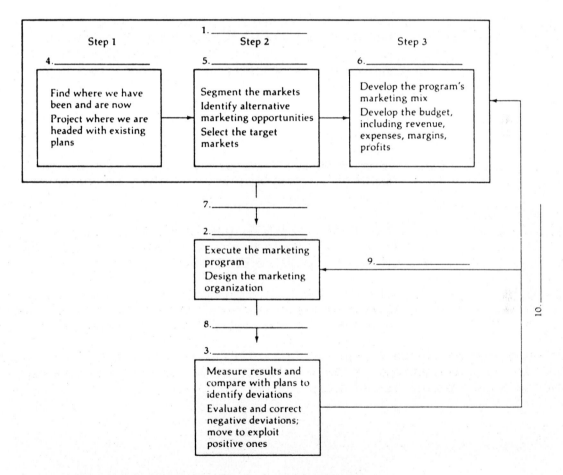

1. _____

Step 1   Step 2   Step 3

4. _____   5. _____   6. _____

Find where we have been and are now Project where we are headed with existing plans	Segment the markets Identify alternative marketing opportunities Select the target markets	Develop the program's marketing mix Develop the budget, including revenue, expenses, margins, profits

7. _____

2. _____

Execute the marketing program
Design the marketing organization

9. _____

8. _____

3. _____

Measure results and compare with plans to identify deviations
Evaluate and correct negative deviations; move to exploit positive ones

10. _____

Fill in the blanks above with the appropriate terms.

Corrective actions	Marketing plan
Corrective actions	Marketing program
Control phase	Planning phase
Goal setting	Results
Implementation phase	Situation analysis

There are three main phases in the strategic marketing process:

> Planning
> Implementation
> Control

I. Match the correct strategic marketing phase to the definitions or statements below.

1. _____The three steps of situation analysis, goal setting, and marketing program development are highly interrelated.

2. _____In this phase, the marketing manager measures the results of the marketing program against the original marketing plan. If there are negative deviations, they are corrected; if there are positive deviations, they are exploited.

3. _____This phase requires carrying out the marketing program and designing the type of marketing organization needed. This is when marketing strategies and tactics are applied.

II.

1. _____Nabisco assigns the responsibility for a new biscuit promotion to a marketing manager. Above him in chain of command is the Group Marketing Manager for biscuits. Below him are the Associate Marketing Manager and the Marketing Assistant.

2. _____Coca-Cola decides to produce products for target markets wanting sugar and/or nonsugar and caffeine and/or noncaffeine products.

3. _____Actual sales for three Kodak Disc camera models in 1983 were less than expected. Kodak pared two models from the line and offered a single basic model for 30 percent less than its predecessor.

ALTERNATIVE MARKETING STRATEGIES

There are four market-product strategies or alternative ways to expand marketing opportunities:

> Market penetration
> Market development
> Product development
> Diversification

I. Match the correct product strategy to the statements below.

1. _____ There is no change in product line offered but increased sales are made possible through better advertising, more retail outlets, and/or lower prices.

2. _____ The product remains the same, but steps are taken to sell to previously untapped markets.

3. _____ This involves developing new products and selling them in new markets.

4. _____ The product changes, but it is sold to existing markets.

5. _____ Tide laundry detergent, sold for years in powder form, now is available in liquid laundry detergent.

6. _____ Proctor & Gamble now manufactures diaper products for adult needs, in addition to manufacturing diapers for babies.

7. _____ TUMS is now sold for its calcium benefits as well as its antacid benefits.

8. _____ In addition to its chemical products, Dow Chemical Canada operates Dow Brands Canada Inc. (Handi-wrap) and Merrell Dow (e.g. Seldane).

S W O T ANALYSIS

The letters in the SWOT acronym stand for:

1. S _____

2. W _____

3. O _____

4. T _____

DISTINCTIVE COMPETENCY

"In assessing organizational opportunities, the firm objectively evaluates its own distinctive competency- its principal competitive strengths and advantages in terms of marketing, technological, and financial resources."

If Kellogg's decided to expand its marketing opportunities, which products or markets would best match its distinctive competency for each of the market-product strategies?

Explain your answers.

1. Market penetration-_____

_____

2. Market development-_____

_____

3. Product development-_____

_____

4. Diversification-_____

_____

PLANNING PHASE

There are three steps in the planning phase of the strategic marketing process:

> Situation analysis
> Goal setting
> Marketing program

Match the correct step in planning to the following definitions or statements.

1. _____ Develop the program's marketing mix and develop the budget including revenue, expenses, margins, and profits.

2. _____ Find where the company has been and where it is now and project where it is heading using the existing plans.

3. _____ Segment the markets, identify alternative marketing opportunities, and select the target markets the firm will address.

SITUATION ANALYSIS

Situation analysis requires a firm to examine both internal and external forces. These include:

Internal	External
Departmental objectives	Competition
Financial resources	Consumer demand
Organizational strengths	Economy
Organizational weaknesses	Political and legal factors
	Technology

Name the factor being considered in each of the following examples.

1. _____ Research showed almost 50 percent of computer systems under $12,000 are sold to small businesses.

2. _____ A recession and high interest rates caused prospective buyers to postpone or skip spending $4000 for a small computer.

3. _____ IBM has a reputation for very good sales and service personnel, plus high brand recognition.

4. _____ IBM had no experience in manufacturing or distributing small personal computers. They also did not have the internal capability to write software programs for their new machine.

5. _____ IBM needed permission to use the Little Tramp character.

6. _____ About 150 firms including Apple, Tandy, and Osborne, were already producing computers.

7. _____ "Develop and market a successful personal computer by 1981."

8. _____ IBM allocated huge sums of money to its new Personal Computer division.

9. _____ IBM must stay abreast of the rapid scientific advancements in lasers because it is very likely that this technology can be applied to personal computers.

TARGET MARKETS

Imagine your company produces toothbrushes. List at least four possible target markets.

1. _____

2. _____

3. _____

4. _____

MARKETING PROGRAM

I. The first step in building a good marketing program is to develop a marketing mix.

Using the example in the text (p. 45-47) for Pampers disposable diapers, check the components you think would be included in the marketing mix.

Product	Price	Promotion	Place
___Features	___List price	___Advertising	___Outlets
___Accessories	___Discounts	___Personal selling	___Channels
___Options	___Allowances	___Sales promotion	___Coverage
___Line breadth	___Credit terms	___Publicity	___Transportation
___Brand name	___Payment period		___Stock level
___Service			
___Warranty			
___Returns			

II.   Step two of the marketing program is developing a budget. Using the Pamper's example (p. 45-47), list at least three questions which should be considered before developing the budget.

1. _____

2. _____

3. _____

STRATEGIC MARKETING PROCESS: IMPLEMENTATION PHASE

Two key elements of the implementation stage are (1) executing the program described in the marketing plan and (2) designing the marketing organization.

Using the information in Chapter 2 regarding Kodak, IBM, or GE, demonstrate the difference between marketing strategies and marketing tactics.

1. Marketing Strategies_____

_____

_____

_____

_____

2. Marketing Tactics_____

_____

_____

_____

_____

STRATEGIC MARKETING PROCESS: CONTROL PHASE

The control phase of the strategic marketing process seeks to keep the marketing program moving in the direction set for it. Accomplishing this requires the marketing manager (1) to compare the results of the marketing program with the goals in the written plans to identify deviations, and (2) to act on these deviations - correcting negative deviations and exploiting positive ones.

The Ocean Spray Cranberries Company has to decide whether to sell its new Mauna La'i Hawaiian Guava Drink nationally or not.

The marketing plan target market was older children through older adults with average income and education.

Goals were set for both "first trial" and "repeat purchases."

Although "first trial" results were good, "repeat purchase" results were not.

Research showed that the highest buyer group was not the targeted market but upscale buyers. (YUPPIES)

Research also showed that upscale buyers consumed larger quantities than expected.

Using the information above, demonstrate your knowledge of the control phase of strategic marketing process. Describe which steps you would take next.

_____

_____

_____

_____

_____

_____

_____

THE STRATEGIC MANAGEMENT AND STRATEGIC MARKETING PROCESS

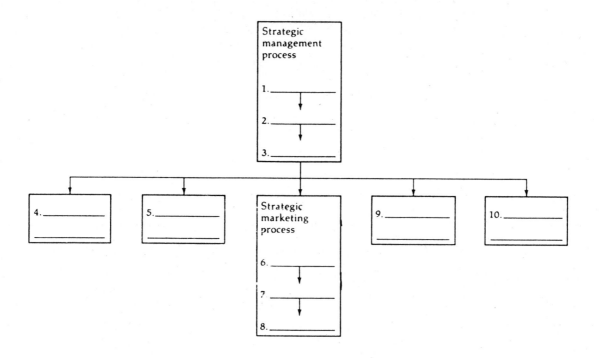

Fill in the blanks with the appropriate terms:

Business (mission)   Manufacturing plan
Control   Objectives
Financial plan   Opportunities
Human resources plan   Planning
Implementation   Research and development

TERMS AND DEFINITIONS

1. strategic marketing process
2. profit
3. planning gap
4. market segmentation
5. business firm
6. distinctive competency
7. market share
8. mission
9. nonprofit organization
10. marketing tactics
11. product cannibalism
12. marketing strategy
13. organizational objectives
14. strategic management process
15. situation analysis
16. goal setting
17. marketing plan
18. product development
19. diversification
20. market development
21. market penetration

BUSINESS (MISSION)

There are many possible correct answers. For further guidance refer to your text page(s): 36

"To market the best racing bicycles in the world."
"To market a lower-priced bicycle with fewer options."
"To market a premium-priced bicycle for the up-scale consumer."

ORGANIZATIONAL GOALS:

1. market share
2. social responsibility
3. profit
4. survival
5. sales revenue
6. unit sales

NON-PROFIT ORGANIZATIONAL GOALS:

There are many possible correct answers. For further guidance refer to your text page(s): 32-36

1. Increase per capita donations.
2. Increase the number of organizations it serves.
3. Increase organizational awareness.
4. Increase corporate sponsorship.
5. Increase number of nonpaid volunteers.

STRATEGIC MARKETING PROCESS
See Figure 2-3 in your text page: 39

1. planning phase
2. implementation phase
3. control phase
4. situation analysis
5. goal setting
6. marketing program
7. marketing plan
8. results
9. corrective actions
10. corrective actions

STRATEGIC MARKETING

1. planning
2. control
3. implementation
4. implementation
5. planning
6. control

ALTERNATIVE MARKETING STRATEGIES

I.

1. market penetration
2. market development
3. diversification
4. product development
5. product development
6. market development
7. market development
8. diversification

SWOT ANALYSIS

1. strengths
2. weaknesses
3. opportunities
4. threats

DISTINCTIVE COMPETENCY

There are many possible correct answers. For further guidance refer to your text page(s): 38

PLANNING PHASE

1. marketing program   2. situational analysis   3. goal setting

SITUATION ANALYSIS

1. consumer demand
2. economy
3. organizational strengths
4. organizational weaknesses
5. political or legal
6. competition
7. departmental objectives
8. financial resources
9. technology

TARGET MARKETS

1. young children
2. teens who want brighter teeth
3. people who travel
4. denture wearers

MARKETING PROGRAM

I. Every one of these answers is correct. Remember that this is an organization which deals with other businesses, not just the consumer. See if you can justify why each category would be included.

II.   1. estimating sales revenue
       2. estimating expenses

STRATEGIC MARKETING PROCESS: IMPLEMENTATION PHASE

There are many possible correct answers.   For further guidance refer to your
text page(s):   47-50

STRATEGIC MARKETING PROCESS: CONTROL PHASE

There are many possible correct answers.   For further guidance refer to your
text page(s):   52-54

QUICK RECALL

1. business (mission)   6.   planning
2. objectives   7.   implementation
3. opportunities   8.   control
4. research and development plan   9.   financial plan
5. manufacturing plan   10. human resources plan

3

THE CHANGING MARKETING ENVIRONMENT

TERMS AND DEFINITIONS

Listed below are the definitions of important marketing terms. Choose the correct term for each definition from the list below, and write it in the space provided.

Baby boomers
Barriers to entry
Blended family
Competition
Consumerism
Culture
Demographics
Discretionary income
Disposable income
Ecology
Economy

Environmental scanning
Gross income
Mature households
Outsourcing
Regional marketing
Regulation
Restructuring
Self-regulation
Single source data
Social forces
Technology

1. _____ The characteristics of the population, its income, and its values.

2. _____ Restrictions provincial and federal laws place on business with regard to the conduct of its activities.

3. _____ The total dollars earned in one year by a person or family unit.

4. _____ Acquiring information on events occurring outside the company and interpreting potential trends.

5. _____ Distribution of a population on selected characteristics such as where people are, their numbers, and who they are in terms of age, sex, income, and occupation.

6. _____ The relationship of physical resources in the environment.

7. _____ A family unit formed by the merging into a single household of two previously separated units.

8. _____ Business practices or conditions that make it difficult for a new product to enter the market.

9. _____ The generation of children born between 1946 and 1964.

10. _____ The set of alternative firms that could provide a product to satisfy a specific market's needs.

11. _____ The set of values, ideas, and attitudes of a homogeneous group of people, that are transmitted from one generation to the next.

12. _____ The money that remains after paying taxes and necessities.

13. _____ An environmental force that includes inventions or innovations from applied science or engineering research.

14. _____ An industry policing itself rather than relying on government controls.

15. _____ The money a consumer has left after paying taxes to use for food, shelter, and clothing.

16. _____ Contracting work that formerly was done in-house by employees in marketing research, advertising, public relations, data processing and training departments, to small outside firms.

17. _____ A movement to increase the influence, power, and rights of consumers in their dealings with institutions.

18. _____ Households headed by people over 50 representing the fastest growing age segment in Canada.

19. _____ The development of marketing plans to reflect specific area differences in taste preference, perceived needs, or interests.

20. _____ The income, expenditures, and resources that affect the cost of running a business and household.

21. _____ Striving for more efficient corporations that can compete globally by selling off unsatisfactory product lines and divisions, closing down unprofitable plants, and laying off employees.

DEMOGRAPHY

"Demography is the study of population and the distribution of its characteristics."

I. Match the following terms with the statements or examples given below.

Baby boomers
CMA (Census Metropolitan Area)
Environmental scanning
Geographic shift
Graying of Canada
Mature households

Regional marketing
Reconstituted (blended) families
Traditional family

1. _____ A geographic component of a labour force of 100,000 or more.

2. _____ The analysis and interpretation of information and trends acquired on events outside the company.

3. _____ The generation of children born between 1946 and 1964. By 1990 they will account for half of all consumer expenditures.

4. _____ Working father, stay-at-home mother, and at least one child. Only 20 percent of today's households are of this type.

5. _____ The family resulting from divorce and remarriage.

6. _____ Canada's birth rate declines and life expectancies increase.

7. _____ Canadians are moving from rural to urban areas.

8. _____ The development of marketing plans to reflect specific area differences in taste preference, perceived needs, or interests.

II. The following examples show how marketing strategies have made use of demography. Which factor do you think most influenced these companies?

Population trend
Baby boom
Canadian family
Geographic shift

1. _____ Procter & Gamble develops Attends adult-size diapers.

2. _____ Victoriaville Furniture manufactures more rectangular tables.

3. _____ Street signs are being made larger and easier to read.

4. _____ Levi-Strauss branches into non-denim clothing.

5. _____ Merrill Lynch puts together a mutual fund called the "Fund for Tomorrow."

6. _____ Apartments are designed with two master bedrooms.

7. _____ An Alberta company opens a distribution center in Toronto.

CULTURE

"The values, ideas, and attitudes of a society as well as the artifacts or symbols of that society transmitted from one generation to another."

Which of the three cultural influences discussed in the text is best demonstrated by the statements below?

Changing role of women
Changing role of men
Change of attitudes

1. _____In 1980, a large percentage of the Canadian population would vote for a qualified woman for Prime Minister.

2. _____A life insurance company places an ad directed to women in a traditional "women's" magazine.

3. _____Nestlés replaces a picture of a woman with that of a man on the label of Taster's Choice decaffeinated coffee.

4. _____Del Monte has added a 14-item product line of no-salt vegetables to appeal to the more health-conscious consumer.

5. _____Placing cents off coupons in male-oriented trade magazines.

6. _____A recent beer commercial depicts young professional women having their own "night out."

ECONOMIC FORCES

"Economy pertains to the economic conditions that affect the cost of business and the consumer's ability to buy goods."

I. Macroeconomics

> Inflation
> Prime rate
> Recession

Match the appropriate term with the definitions or statements below.

1. _____The rate of interest charged by banks to their largest customers (usually corporations).

2. _____Price levels increase more rapidly than income.

3. _____This reduces the number of items a consumer can buy as prices of products rise.

4. _____Because of this, businesses decrease production and unemployment usually rises.

5. _____Consumers develop a "buy now" attitude because of anticipated price increases.

6. _____Consumers have less money to spend.

II. Consumer Income

Mr. Jones earns $36,000 a year divided into equal payments. His monthly paychecks list the following deductions:

> Federal taxes $550
> Provincial taxes   150
> Canada Pension Plan   250

He pays his bills monthly. His average expenses are:

Rent	$500	Food	$350
Utilities	150	Clothing	100
Medical	50	Insurance	50
Transportation	50		

1. What is his gross monthly income?_____

2. What is his monthly disposable income?_____

3. What is his monthly discretionary income?_____

4. What percent of his gross income does his discretionary income

   represent? _____

TECHNOLOGY

I. What technological development(s) affected the following products?

1. Straight razor _____

2. Slide ruler _____

3. Radio tubes _____

4. Nylons _____

5. Carbon paper _____

6. Typewriters _____

II. Two areas of technology which promise to have a significant impact on marketing are biotechnology and advanced materials.

Define and give a specific example for each.

1. _____

_____

_____

_____

2. _____

_____

_____

_____

COMPETITION

"Competition refers to the set of alternative producers that provide a product that can satisfy a specific market's needs."

I. There are four basic types of competition.

> Pure competition
> Monopolistic competition
> Oligopoly
> Monopoly

Which form of competition best fits the statements below?

1. _____ This form of competition has unique but substitutable products.

2. _____ This form of competition has unique and unsubstitutable products.

3. _____ In this form of competition firms have indistinguishable products.

4. _____ In this form of competition there are a large number of sellers.

5. _____ In this form of competition there are usually only a few large competitors.

6. _____ In this form of competition there are similar products.

7. _____ In this form of competition there is a single producer.

II.

1. _____ In this form of competition, pricing is especially important.

2. _____ In this form of competition distribution is especially important.

3. _____ In this form of competition promotion is key to achieving product difference.

4. _____ In this form of competition, marketing has only limited significance.

III. If the price of pure refined white sugar became too high, list at least eight "substitutes."

1. _____ 5. _____

2. _____ 6. _____

3. _____ 7. _____

4. _____ 8. _____

COMPETITIVE ENVIRONMENT

There are five main forces to monitor in the competitive environment:

> Barriers to entry
> Substitutes
> Power of buyers
> Power of suppliers
> Existing competition

I.   Match the term to the correct definition:

1. _____The competitive power of this group is increased when there are low switching costs, the product represents a significant share of the consumer's costs, or sales are concentrated among only a few consumers.

2. _____When the price of a given product becomes unreasonably high, the consumer or buyer finds an alternate way of satisfying his needs.

3. _____Pressures vary as a function of industry growth, the proportion of fixed costs, and the level of product identity.

4. _____A firm assesses the likelihood of new competitors. Difficulties exist for potential competitors because of capital requirements, advertising expenditures, access to distributors, switching costs, and product identity.

5. _____This group can have a significant effect when their product is critical to the buyer and when they have built up switching costs.

II.   Match the factor in the competitive environment to the appropriate statements below:

> Barriers to entry
> Substitutes
> Power of buyers
> Power of suppliers
> Existing competition

1. _____When coffee prices skyrocketed, people began buying more tea and cocoa.

2. _____A research project shows Gerber has a 99 percent brand awareness rate. Three out of four respondents stated a preference for the brand.

3. _____Each year 20,000 families convert their homes to solar energy.

4. _____The owner/operator of an earthworm farm located near six famous fishing lakes is the only supplier of worms in a five-county area.

5. _____ For years Avis has been touting its "number two" position in the rental car industry.

6. _____ Because of an exclusive patent and a revolutionary manufacturing process, Intel is the sole producer of a special chip that is a necessary component in microcomputers.

7. _____ The Bay Department Store reduced the number of types of dolls it displayed by half, to make room for Cabbage Patch Kids.

8. _____ In 1985 Apple changed its emphasis from home computers to office computers to compete with IBM for the business market.

9. _____ A major retailer plans to purchase 400,000 lawn mowers from two lawn mower manufacturers and sell them under its own private label.

10. _____ The Canadian government is planning to purchase a number of nuclear submarines. Several companies are vying for the contract.

11. _____ It costs $400 million to build a brewery that will produce 100 barrels of beer per day.

BARRIERS TO ENTRY

There are five barriers to entry. Barriers to entry are business practices or conditions that make it difficult for new firms to enter the market. They include:

Capital requirements
Advertising expenditures
Access to distributors
Switching costs
Product identity

Match the "barrier" to the appropriate statement below.

1. _____ A manufacturer of disposable diapers wishes to compete with Huggies, Pampers, and Luvs.

2. _____ Promotion that used to cost in the tens of thousands now costs as much as $25 million because of the licensing of toys (using names and/or likenesses of movie characters, etc.).

3. _____ A Canadian Greeting card company supplies its independent retailers with display fixtures at no cost with the "understanding" that only their products can be displayed on them.

4. _____ One of the first and most popular home video games only played cartridges manufactured by its company.

5. _____ Initial plant and equipment outlays for new companies entering the field of automobile manufacturing are astronomical.

6. _____ In most supermarket chains, Kraft products dominate dairy-case space.

7. _____ You cannot use the same software disks on Apple and IBM microcomputers.

8. _____ A grocery store displays its generic brand at eye level (i.e., the preferred shelf location) throughout the store.

9. _____ A major softdrink manufacturer hired Michael Jackson to star in a series of high-powered, prime-time, television commercials.

10. _____ A local artist wishes to enter the direct mail market; the price difference between his current black and white brochures and a four colour glossy is over $1,000 just for production costs.

REGULATION

"Regulation is the laws placed on a business with regard to the conduct of its activities."

I.   The Competition Act, designed to protect and balance the interests of competitors and consumers, contains criminal and non-criminal (reviewable) provisions. Identify whether the following are <u>criminal (c)</u> or <u>reviewable (r)</u> under the Competition Act by putting a C or R next to the following:

1. _____Price-Fixing

2. _____Refusal to Deal

3. _____Tied selling

4. _____Price maintenance

5. _____Mergers

    *Challenge - Call your local Better Business Bureau and find out what information they provide and what information is available for a company of your choice.

I. List the five forces that drive competition:

    1. _____

    2. _____

    3. _____

    4. _____

    5. _____

II. List two important social factors which influence marketing decisions:

    1. _____

    2. _____

III. List two important economic forces which influence marketing decisions:

    1. _____

    2. _____

IV. List three types of consumer income:

    1. _____

    2. _____

    3. _____

V. List two important technological factors which influence marketing decisions:

    1. _____

    2. _____

VI. List three factors of competition which influence marketing decisions:

    1. _____

    2. _____

    3. _____

VII.   List the four different forms of competition:

1. _____

2. _____

3. _____

4. _____

VIII. List five forces that drive competition:

1. _____

2. _____

3. _____

4. _____

5. _____

IX.   List five possible barriers to entry:

1. _____

2. _____

3. _____

4. _____

5. _____

TERMS AND DEFINITIONS

1. social forces
2. regulation
3. gross income
4. environmental scanning
5. demographics
6. ecology
7. blended families
8. barriers to entry
9. baby boomers
10. competition
11. culture

12. discretionary income
13. technology
14. self-regulation
15. disposable income
16. outsourcing
17. consumerism
18. mature households
19. regional marketing
20. economy
21. restructuring

DEMOGRAPHY

I. 1. CMA
    2. environmental scanning
    3. baby boomers
    4. Changing role of men

    5. reconstituted (blended) families
    6. graying of Canada
    7. geographic shift
    8. regional marketing

II. 1. population trend
    2. Canadian family
    3. population trend
    4. baby boom

    5. baby boom
    6. Canadian family
    7. geographic shift

CULTURE

1. attitudes
2. women
3. men
4. attitudes
5. men
6. women

ECONOMIC FORCES

I. Economy Macroeconomics

1. prime rate
2. inflation
3. inflation
4. recession
5. inflation
6. recession

II. Consumer income

1. $3,000   2. $2,050   3. $800   4. 26.67 percent

TECHNOLOGY

I There are many possible correct answers. For further guidance refer to your text page(s): 71-74

1. electric shaver, disposable razors, depilatories
2. calculators, home computers
3. transistors
4. pantyhose
5. photo copiers, mimeograph machines, computer printers
6. word processors

II See pages 72-73

COMPETITION

I.
1. monopolistic competition
2. monopoly
3. pure competition
4. monopolistic competition/ pure competition
5. oligopoly
6. oligopoly / monopolistic competition
7. monopoly

II.
1. monopolistic competition

2. pure competition

3. oligopoly

4. monopoly

III. There are many possible correct answers. For further guidance refer to your text page(s): 75-76.

1. brown sugar
2. honey
3. molasses
4. saccharin
5. NutraSweet
6. corn syrup
7. fresh fruit
8. no sweetener at all

COMPETITIVE ENVIRONMENT

I.
1. power of buyers
2. substitutes
3. existing competition
4. barriers to entry
5. power of suppliers

II.
1. substitutes
2. barriers to entry
3. substitutes
4. power of suppliers
5. competition
6. power of suppliers
7. competition or barriers to entry
8. competition
9. power of buyers
10. power of buyers
11. barriers to entry

BARRIERS TO ENTRY

1. advertising or product identity
2. advertising expenditures
3. access to distributors
4. switching costs
5. capital requirements

6. access to distributors
7. switching costs
8. access to distributors
9. advertising
10. capital requirements

REGULATION

I   1. criminal
    2. reviewable
    3. reviewable
    4. criminal
    5. reviewable

QUICK RECALL

I.   1. social
     2. economic
     3. technological
     4. competitive
     5. regulatory

II. 1. demographics
     2. culture

III. 1. macroeconomic conditions
     2. consumer income

IV. 1. gross
     2. disposable
     3. discretionary

V.   1. future of technology
     2. ecological impact of technology

VI. 1. alternative competitive forms
     2. components of competition
     3. increasing foreign competition

VII. 1. pure competition
     2. monopolistic competition
     3. oligopoly
     4. monopoly

VIII. 1. power of buyers
      2. power of suppliers
      3. barriers to entry
      4. substitutes
      5. existing competition

IX. 1. advertising
     2. product identity
     3. switching costs
     4. capital requirements
     5. access to distributers

4

CONSUMER BEHAVIOUR

TERMS AND DEFINITIONS

Listed below are the definitions of important marketing terms. Choose the correct term for each definition from the list below, and write it in the space provided.

Attitude
Beliefs
Brand loyalty
Cognitive dissonance
Consumer behaviour
Consumer socialization
Evaluative criteria
Evoked set
Family Life Cycle
Involvement
Learning
Life-style
Motivation

Opinion leaders
Perceived risk
Perception
Personality
Purchase decision process
Reference groups
Self concept
Situational influences
Social class
Subculture
Values
Word-of-mouth

1. _____ Relatively permanent, homogeneous divisions in a society in which people sharing similar values, interests, and behaviour can be grouped.

2. _____ A situation's effect on the nature and scope of the purchase decision process.

3. _____ Steps or stages a buyer passes through in making choices about which products and services to buy.

4. _____ People to whom an individual turns as a standard of self-appraisal or source of personal standards.

5. _____ The anxieties felt because the consumer cannot anticipate the outcomes of a purchase but believes that there may be negative consequences.

6. _____ The concept that each family progresses through a number of distinct phases and each phase brings with it identifiable purchasing behaviors.

7. _____ The process by which an individual selects, organizes, and interprets information to create a meaningful picture of the world.

8. _____ Person's enduring or consistent psychological traits, such as extroversion, aggression, or compliance.

9. _____ Subgroups within the larger or national culture with unique values, ideas, and attitudes.

10. _____ Those behaviors that result from repeated experience and thinking.

11. _____ Consumers' subjective perception of how well a product or brand performs on different attributes.

12. _____ The group of brands that a consumer would consider buying out of the set of brands in the product class of which he or she is aware.

13. _____ Process by which people acquire the skills, knowledge, and attitudes necessary to function as consumers.

14. _____ A favorable attitude toward, and a consistent purchase of, a single brand over time.

15. _____ The feeling of postpurchase psychological tension or anxiety.

16. _____ Mode of living identified by an individual's activities, interests, and opinions.

17. _____ Both the objective attributes and the subjective factors important to consumers when making a purchase decision.

18. _____ Learned predisposition to respond to an object or class of objects in a consistently favorable or unfavorable way.

19. _____ Actions of a person to purchase and use products and services.

20. _____ The personal and economic significance of the purchase to the consumer.

21. _____ The energizing force that causes behaviour that satisfies a need.

22. _____ Individuals who exert direct or indirect social influence over others.

23. _____ The way people see themselves and the way they believe others see them.

24. _____ Personally or socially preferable modes of conduct or states of existence that are enduring.

25. _____ People influencing each other during their face-to-face conversations.

PURCHASE DECISION PROCESS

"The <u>sequential</u> steps or stages a consumer passes through in making choices about which products and services to buy are called the <u>purchase decision process</u>."

The sequential steps are:

> Problem recognition
> Information seeking
> Alternative evaluation
> Purchase decision
> Postpurchase evaluation

Match the following statements to the correct step in the purchase decision process.

I.

1. _____ I'm glad I didn't buy the scented tissues; they would have irritated my allergies.

2. _____ I'm tired of washing handkerchiefs; I need something more convenient.

3. _____ I can't decide between a designer box, convenience pack, or scented or unscented tissues.

4. _____ Can you tell me which kind of tissue you like best?

5. _____ I'm going to buy these, thank you.

II.

1. _____ The price of fresh produce at the grocery store is too expensive.

2. _____ The cost of topsoil runs $50 for 8 cubic yards, and railroad ties cost almost $8 apiece. I could just rent a plot from the Parks Department. Gardening may be more trouble than it's worth.

3. _____ Please deliver the dirt and ties on Saturday; just charge them to my account.

4. _____ Is there anything to compare with these home grown vegetables? I don't think so. They taste so much better.

5. _____ You have a garden. Is it worth the time and effort? How much time does it take? What did your dirt and seeds cost?

INFORMATION SEARCH

There are two main types of information search:

1. Internal search - The consumer relies on prior experience or knowledge. Usually used for frequently purchased low-value items.

   e.g. experience

2. External search - Usually used when past knowledge is insufficient, risk of an incorrect decision is high, and cost of gathering information is low.

   e.g. Personal sources
   Public sources
   Marketer-dominated sources

Read the statements below. Decide if each reflects an internal or external search resource. If the statement is "external," specify which <u>type</u> of external search resource is being used.

1. _____ Mom, can you tell me which dress you think
   _____ looks better?

2. _____ The local television listings rate movies on a
   _____ four-star system.

3. _____ I've been using the same brand of paint for
   _____ years and have been very satisfied.

4. _____ Come and take a test drive - see how the
   _____ car handles on the open highway.

5. _____ As far as I'm concerned, all white bread tastes
   _____ the same.

6. _____ The store ad in the "Yellow Pages" tells
   _____ everything from brands serviced to store hours
   to special senior citizen discounts.

7. _____ Before making any major appliance purchase I
   _____ almost always consult "Consumer Reports".

8. _____ Before doing business with a new firm I like
   _____ to check with the Better Business Bureau.

9. _____ According to the instructions on the
   _____ package, everything I need is included.

ALTERNATIVE EVALUATION

"The information search stage serves to clarify the <u>options</u> available to the consumer. The evoked set is the subset of brands that a consumer would consider buying out of the set of brands in the product class of which he or she is aware."

I.   List all members of <u>your</u> evoked set for <u>one</u> of the following products. Choose an item with at least five (5) alternatives.

Automobile	Breakfast cereal
Paper towels	Candy bars
Laundry detergents	Shoes

Example:

Evoked Set:

Dish soap:
1. <u>Dawn</u>

2. <u>Ivory</u>

3. <u>Dove</u>

4. <u>Joy</u>

5. <u>Ajax</u>

Evoked Set:

<u>Product</u>:
1._____

2._____

3._____

4._____

5._____

II. Consumers use <u>valuative criteria</u> to make decisions. Product attributes are evaluated objectively and subjectively.

A.   Decide whether the following consumer statements describe objective (O) or subjective (S) valuative criteria.

1._____The suds last longer.
2._____The suds cut grease.
3._____This bottle costs 25 percent less.
4._____This smells better.
5._____There are 4 ounces more per bottle.
6._____The top pops off when you squeeze the bottle.
7._____My mother always uses this.
8._____This brand contains a hand cream.

B. Using the evoked set you identified previously, make lists of subjective and objective valuative criteria for your product. (Find as many as possible).

<table>
<tr><td>**OBJECTIVE**</td><td>**SUBJECTIVE**</td></tr>
<tr><td>1._____</td><td>1._____</td></tr>
<tr><td>2._____</td><td>2._____</td></tr>
<tr><td>3._____</td><td>3._____</td></tr>
<tr><td>4._____</td><td>4._____</td></tr>
<tr><td>5._____</td><td>5._____</td></tr>
</table>

PURCHASE DECISION

"Having examined the alternatives in the evoked set, the consumer makes a purchase decision. This actual decision is not often observable by marketers..."

"The purchase decision is expected to follow as a consequence of what occurred in the consumer's mind during the alternative evaluation stage. But this does not always happen."

These purchase decisions are called impulsive purchase decisions.

Identify the last impulsive purchase decision you made. Describe the conditions surrounding your purchase.

_____

_____

_____

_____

POSTPURCHASE BEHAVIOUR

"Many times after making a purchase a consumer experiences a postpurchase psychological tension or anxiety called cognitive dissonance."

A consumer may deal with cognitive dissonance by one of the following methods:

    A.   Search for information to confirm the choice or search for advertisements of the chosen brand only.

B.   Negatively reevaluate the rejected alternative.

C.   In the case of a commitment to purchase preceding the actual purchase itself, firms often use ads or follow-ups by salespeople to try to convince buyers they made the right decision.

Which method (A, B, or C) is being demonstrated in the statement below?

1.   _____"Aren't you glad you use Dial?"

2.   _____That other brand is far less fuel efficient.

3.   _____"You're going to love your new neighborhood."

4.   _____According to this article, that other camera doesn't have one redeeming quality.

5.   _____This is the same dress I saw someone wearing at the Academy Awards.

6.   _____"Wouldn't you really rather drive a Buick?"

INVOLVEMENT

"Involvement refers to the personal and economic significance of the purchase to the consumer."

High-Involvement
Low-Involvement

Decide which of the following purchases would most likely be considered high-involvement purchases, and which would most likely be considered low-involvement purchases.

1.   _____   automobile
2.   _____   daycare
3.   _____   underwear
4.   _____   motor oil
5.   _____   shampoo
6.   _____   breakfast cereal

PROBLEM-SOLVING VARIATIONS

"Three general variations in the consumer purchase decision process exist." They are:

Routine problem solving
Limited problem solving
Extended problem solving

Match the correct process with the statements below.

1. _____Limited external information search is conducted to identify alternatives and important attributes.

2. _____This is used with widely available products of low unit value and high familiarity.

3. _____This process would be used with items such as toothpaste or chewing gum.

4. _____This involves each stage of the consumer purchase decision process.

5. _____This process would likely be used for clothing, popcorn poppers, electric can openers.

6. _____This process would likely be used for real estate, automobiles, personal computers.

SITUATIONAL INFLUENCES

"Five situational factors have been identified as having an impact on the decision process." They are:

> Purchase task
> Social surroundings
> Physical surroundings
> Temporal effects
> Antecedent states

Match the situational factors to the statements below.

1. _____The store aisles are cluttered and crowded.

2. _____This is for my mother-in-law.

3. _____Gosh, I left my wallet at home.

4. _____The store is closing; we better make up our mind.

5. _____Mom, what do you think?

6. _____I only have $1000 for a down payment on an automobile.

7. _____The air conditioning is broken.

8. _____I worked hard for this money. I'm going to buy something special for myself.

9. _____They don't make hamburgers until 10:30 a.m. at this restaurant.

10. _____I'm not going to buy that while you're here.

PSYCHOLOGICAL INFLUENCES ON THE CONSUMER PURCHASE DECISION PROCESS

MOTIVATION

"Motivation is the energizing force that causes behaviour to satisfy a need."

There are four need classes:

> Physiological
> Safety
> Social
> Personal

Which need would best be described by the following statements?

1. _____ Bread is the staff of life.

2. _____ "You're in good hands with Allstate."

3. _____ "... when you care enough to give the very best."

4. _____ "You're the Pepsi Generation."

PERCEPTION

I. Selective perception

"Because the average consumer operates in a complex environment, the human brain attempts to organize and interpret the world through a four-stage filtering system. This selective perceptual process involves:

> Selective exposure
> Selective attention
> Selective comprehension
> Selective retention

Match the type of selective perception with the appropriate statements below.

1. _____Consumers do not <u>remember</u> all the information they see, read, or hear.

2. _____Consumers <u>pay attention</u> to messages that are consistent with their attitudes and beliefs and <u>ignore</u> messages that are inconsistent.

3. _____"The ad said something about a warranty, but I'm not sure if they said they had one or didn't have one."

4. _____"People thought Toro's SnowPup was a toy or too lightweight to do snow blowing even though it could do the job."

5. _____"I'm glad I bought my home through this realty company; I see their signs everywhere."

II. Perceived risk

"Perceived risk represents the anxieties inherent in a purchase in which the consumer cannot anticipate the outcomes, but perceives that the outcomes might have negative consequences."

There are several factors that generate perceived risk:

> Financial outlay
> Physical harm
> Performance of the product
> Psychosocial factors

Companies have used many strategies to reduce customer anxieties. Which factor of perceived risk is being addressed in the following statements?

1. _____Ford advertisements stated that "quality" was "job one."

2. _____A Black & Decker circular saw displays the CSA seal.

3. _____Carolyn Waldo endorses Sears's line of women's clothing.

4. _____Free trial offers and/or small-sized packages of a new conditioning shampoo are sent through the mail.

5. _____The instructions with each Weed Eater advise buyers to wear safety glasses while using the product.

6. _____Chrysler gives warranties to its automobile drive trains and transmissions for 7 years or 115,000 kilometers.

7. _____Only the finest students are enrolled in this school.

8. _____When your boss says the package has to be in Toronto tomorrow, Purolator says, ". . . when its just got to be there".

*Challenge - For each of the above examples, assess how effective you think the risk-reduction strategy was.

LEARNING

I. Behaviour learning

A. "Learning refers to those behaviors which result from experience."

Four variables are central to the learning process:

> Drive
> Cues
> Response
> Reinforcement

Match the learning variable to the correct statement.

1. _____A person turns on a gas grill and gets steaks from the freezer.

2. _____A person is hungry.

3. _____The aroma of charcoal-grilled steaks floats over from next door.

4. _____A person slices into a thick, juicy, rare steak, eats it, and smiles.

5. _____A person sprays an analgesic on his sunburn.

6. _____A person lies out in the sun too long and begins to itch and burn.

7. _____The itching and pain begin to recede.

8. _____A person sees a commercial for a sunburn spray.

B. Two important concepts have emerged from behaviour learning theory:

Stimulus generalization
Stimulus discrimination

Match the behaviour learning theory concept to the correct statement.

1. _____Weight Watchers, in addition to having a well known weight loss program, also distributes a line of frozen foods, desserts, and cookbooks.

2. _____Mr. Big uses the slogan "When you're this Big, they call you Mister."

3. _____Diet Coke uses the slogan "You're gonna drink it just for the taste of it".

4. _____Black and Decker makes power tools and small kitchen appliances and sells them under the Black and Decker name.

II. Cognitive learning

"Cognitive learning involves making connections between two or more ideas or simply observing the outcomes of others' behaviours and adjusting one's own accordingly."

"Learning is also important because it relates to habit formation ..."

There is a close link between habits and <u>brand loyalty</u>.

Make a list of five products towards which you have "brand loyalty." List the reasons you have for making these choices.

1._____

2._____

3._____

4._____

5._____

VALUES, BELIEFS, AND ATTITUDES

A. "Attitudes are shaped by our values and beliefs which also are learned."

"Personal values affect attitude by influencing the importance assigned to specific product attributes."

"Beliefs are consumers' subjective perception of how well a product performs on different attributes."

Values
Beliefs

Which of the following statements reflect an attitude affected by a person's values, and which statements reflect an attitude affected by a person's belief?

1. _____My mother always said Hellman's was the smoothest mayonnaise.

2. _____Reliability, not style, is the most important function of a good watch.

3. _____I will never understand how someone can purchase one of those luxury cars; those cars are so wasteful of fuel compared to economy cars.

4. _____Based on past experience, I think Apple is the easiest computer to use.

   B. "Marketers frequently use three approaches to try to change consumer attitudes toward products and brands."

   1. Change beliefs about the extent to which a brand has certain attributes.

   2. Change the perceived importance of attributes.

   3. Add new attributes.

Using current advertisements, find two examples for each of the three ways in which marketers may influence attitudes.

_____

_____

_____

_____

_____

_____

LIFESTYLE

   "Lifestyle analysis (also called psychographics) has produced many insights into why and how consumers purchase products and services."

The "VALS Program" has identified four categories of adult life styles that relate to the behaviour of segments of consumers.

Need driven people
Inner-directed people
Outer-directed people
Integrated people

Match the type of life-style to the correct description.

1. _____ Are concerned with financial security
2. _____ Adhere to social norms and value appearances
3. _____ Emphasize quality, uniqueness and esthetics
4. _____ Seek self-expression and pursue individual needs

SOCIOCULTURAL INFLUENCES ON CONSUMER BEHAVIOUR

"The effects of sociocultural influences are examined in terms of personal influence, reference groups, the family, social class, culture, and subculture."

PERSONAL INFLUENCES

"Two aspects of personal influence are important to marketing: opinion leadership and word-of-mouth activity."

Opinion leadership
Word-of-mouth activity

Match the type of personal influence to the correct statement below:

1. _____ This type of influence is more likely to be important for products that provide a form of self expression.

2. _____ Celebrities and sports figures are often used as spokespeople.

3. _____ Perhaps the most powerful information source for consumers.

4. _____ A form of one-way directed influence.

5. _____ "Teaser" advertising and toll free numbers are sometimes used.

REFERENCE GROUPS

"Reference groups are people to whom an individual looks as a basis for self-appraisal or as a source of personal standards."

There are three important reference groups with marketing implications:

> Membership group
> Aspiration group
> Avoidance group

Match the reference group to the correct statement:

I.

1. _____   A group to which a person actually belongs.

2. _____   A group a person wishes to be identified with.

3. _____   A group a person wishes to maintain a distance from due to differences in values or behaviour.

FAMILY INFLUENCE

I. Family life cycle

List the seven different classifications or stages in the family life cycle.

1. _____

2. _____

3. _____

4. _____

5. _____

6. _____

7. _____

II. Family decision-making

There are two common decision-making styles:

Spouse dominant
Joint decision-making

Which decision-making style is demonstrated by the following statement?

1. _____ "I'm the one who does all the laundry; I should decide what model washer to buy."

2. _____ "Let's look over all the brochures and we'll decide where we want to take our vacation."

III. Roles in Family Decision-Making

Five roles exist in the family decision-making process:

Information gatherer
Influencer
Decision-maker
Purchaser
User

Describe a situation where the following people could play each of the 5 roles in the family decision-making process. (Be sure to identify the product).

1. Wife

_____

_____

_____

_____

_____

2. Teenaged son

_____

_____

_____

_____

_____

3. Eight-year old daughter

_____

_____

_____

_____

_____

QUICK RECALL

INFLUENCES ON THE CONSUMER PURCHASE DECISION PROCESS

Fill in the blanks below with the missing components.

Marketing Mix Influences

I. 1._____   2._____   3._____   4._____

Psychological Influences	Consumer Purchase Decision Process	Sociocultural Influences

II. 1._____   III. 1._____   IV. 1._____

     2._____   2._____   2._____

     3._____   3._____   3._____

     4._____   4._____   4._____

     5._____   5._____   5._____

Situational influences

V. 1._____   2._____   3._____   4._____   5._____

TERMS AND DEFINITIONS

1. social class
2. situational influences
3. purchase decision process
4. reference group
5. perceived risk
6. family life cycle
7. perception
8. personality
9. subculture
10. learning
11. beliefs
12. evoked set
13. consumer socialization
14. brand loyalty
15. cognitive dissonance
16. life-style
17. valuative criteria
18. attitudes
19. consumer behaviour
20. involvement
21. motivation
22. opinion leaders
23. self concept
24. values
25. word-of-mouth

PURCHASE DECISION PROCESS

I.
1. postpurchase evaluation
2. problem recognition
3. alternative evaluation
4. information seeking
5. purchase decision

II.
1. problem recognition
2. alternative evaluation
3. purchase decision
4. postpurchase evaluation
5. information seeking

INFORMATION SEARCH

1. external personal
2. external public
3. internal
4. external experience
5. internal
6. external marketer dominated
7. external public
8. external public
9. external marketer dominated

ALTERNATIVE EVALUATION

I. There are many possible correct answers. For further guidance refer to your text page(s): 94.

II. A.
1. Subjective
2. Objective
3. Objective
4. Subjective
5. Objective
6. Objective
7. Subjective
8. Objective

B. There are many possible correct answers. For further guidance refer to your text page(s): 94.

PURCHASE DECISION

There are many possible correct answers. For further guidance refer to your text page(s): 94.

POSTPURCHASE BEHAVIOUR

1. a
2. b

3. c
4. b

5. a
6. c or a

INVOLVEMENT

1. high-involvement
2. high-involvement
3. low-involvement
4. low-involvement
5. low-involvement
6. low-involvement

PROBLEM-SOLVING VARIATIONS

1. limited problem solving
2. routine problem solving
3. routine problem solving

4. extended problem solving
5. limited problem solving
6. extended problem solving

SITUATIONAL INFLUENCES

1. physical surroundings
2. purchase task
3. antecedent states
4. temporal effects
5. social surroundings

6. antecedent states
7. physical surroundings
8. purchase task
9. temporal effects
10. social surroundings

PSYCHOLOGICAL INFLUENCES ON THE CONSUMER PURCHASE DECISION PROCESS

MOTIVATION

1. physiological
2. safety
3. personal
4. social

PERCEPTION

I. Selective perception

1. selective retention
2. selective attention
3. selective comprehension

4. selective comprehension
5. selective exposure

II. Perceived risk

1. performance
2. physical harm
3. social or psychological
4. financial outlay

5. physical harm
6. financial outlay
7. social or psychological
8. performance

LEARNING

I. A

1. response
2. drive
3. cue
4. reinforcement

5. response
6. drive
7. reinforcement
8. cue

I. B

1. stimulus generalization
2. stimulus discrimination
3. stimulus discrimination
4. stimulus generalization

II. There are many possible correct answers. For further guidance refer to your text page(s): 102-103.

VALUES, BELIEFS, AND ATTITUDES

A.

1. beliefs
2. values
3. values
4. beliefs

B.

There are many possible correct answers. For further guidance refer to your text page(s): 104.

LIFE-STYLE

1. Need-driven
2. Outer-directed
3. Integrated
4. Inner-driven

SOCIOCULTURAL INFLUENCES

PERSONAL INFLUENCE

1. opinion leadership
2. opinion leadership
3. word-of-mouth
4. opinion leadership
5. word-of-mouth

REFERENCE GROUPS

I.

1. membership group
2. aspiration group
3. avoidance group

FAMILY AFFLUENCE

I FAMILY LIFE CYCLE

1. young singles
2. young marrieds without children
3. young marrieds with children
4. middle-aged marrieds with children
5. middle-aged marrieds without children
6. older marrieds
7. older unmarrieds

II. FAMILY DECISION-MAKING

1. spouse dominant
2. joint decision making

III. There are many possible correct answers. For further guidance refer to your text page(s): 109-110.

QUICK RECALL

I.
1. product
2. price
3. promotion
4. place

II.
1. learning
2. motivation
3. perception
4. attitudes
5. life style

III.
1. problem recognition
2. information search
3. alternative evaluation
4. purchase decision
5. postpurchase evaluation

IV.
1. family
2. reference group
3. social class
4. culture
5. subculture
6. personal influence

V.
1. purchase task
2. social surroundings
3. physical surroundings
4. temporal effects
5. antecedent states

5

INDUSTRIAL AND ORGANIZATIONAL BUYER BEHAVIOUR

TERMS AND DEFINITIONS

Listed below are the definitions of important marketing terms. Choose the correct term for each definition from the list below, and write it in the space provided.

Bidders list
Buy classes
Buying center
Buying objectives
Derived demand
Industrial firms
Government units
Make-buy decision
Modified rebuy

New buy
Organizational buyers
Organizational buying behaviour
Organizational buying criteria
Reciprocity
Resellers
Standard Industrial Classification (SIC) System
Straight rebuy
Value analysis

1. _____ The reordering of an existing product or service from the list of acceptable suppliers, generally without checking with the various users or influencers.

2. _____ A systematic appraisal of the design, quality, and performance requirements of a product to reduce purchasing costs.

3. _____ Goals set by the participants of the buying process to help them achieve their organization's objectives.

4. _____ An organizational buyer that in some way reprocesses a product or service they buy before selling it to the next buyer.

5. _____ A buying situation in which the users, influencers, or deciders change the product specifications, price, delivery schedule, or supplier.

6. _____ The group of individuals within an organization who participate in the buying process and share common goals, risks, and knowledge important to a purchase decision.

7. _____ An evaluation of whether or not a product or its parts will be purchased from outside suppliers or built by the firm.

8. _____ Business firms and nonprofit organizations that buy goods and services and then resell them with or without reprocessing to other organizations or ultimate consumers.

9. _____ The group of three specific buying situations organizations face: new buy, straight rebuy, and modified rebuy.

10. _____ A list of firms believed to be qualified to supply a given item.

11. _____ Federal, provincial, and local agencies that buy goods and services for the constituents they serve.

12. _____ The first-time purchase of a product or service characterized by greater potential risk.

13. _____ Wholesalers or retailers who buy physical products and resell them again without any processing.

14. _____ The federal government's system of classifying organizations on the basis of major activity or the major good or service provided.

15. _____ The decision-making process that organizations use to establish the need for products and services, and identify, evaluate, and choose among alternative brands and suppliers.

16. _____ The objective attributes of the supplier's products and services and the capabilities of the supplier itself.

17. _____ An industrial buying practice in which two organizations agree to purchase each others products and services.

18. _____ The demand for industrial products and services is driven by or derived from demand for consumer products and services.

ORGANIZATIONAL BUYERS

"Organizational buyers are business firms and non-profit establishments that buy goods and services and then resell them with or without reprocessing to other organizations or ultimate consumers."

Organizational buyers are divided into three different markets:

> Industrial markets
> Reseller markets
> Government markets

Match the correct organizational buyer market with the statements below:

1. _____ The mayor's secretary orders a gross of paper clips for office use.

2. _____ Bank of Montreal and Merrill Lynch decide to buy and use the yellow Post-It note pads in their offices.

3. _____ Coca-Cola buys NutraSweet to use in its Diet Coke.

4. _____ A farmer orders seeds for the coming planting season.

5. _____ Eaton's purchases food dehydrators from ABC Food Systems.

6. _____ Lucite sells "Quick Metal" to maintenance shops from many diverse industries.

7. _____ The City of Toronto places an order with Scott for over 100,000 rolls of toilet tissue.

8. _____ A large metropolitan firm hires Ernst & Young to do its accounting.

9. _____ The Saint John Shipyards is building new ships for the Canadian Navy.

10. _____ A gourmet restaurant buys fresh herbs to use in cooking.

"The SIC system groups organizations on the basis of major activity or the major product or service provided."

I. List two advantages of the SIC system.

    1. _____

    2. _____

    List two disadvantages of the SIC system.

    3. _____

    4. _____

CHARACTERISTICS OF ORGANIZATIONAL BUYING

BUYING CRITERIA

I.

Seven of the most important buying criteria organizations use include:

> Price
> Quality
> Delivery
> Technical capability
> Warranties
> Past performance
> Production facilities and capacity.

Rank the criteria you think would be most important (1 = highest) in purchasing these products for the given firms. (Choose your top 3). Provide a justification for your rankings.

A. Product: Toilet paper

LUXURY HOTEL	SMALL CONSTRUCTION FIRM	VANCOUVER PUBLIC SCHOOLS
1. _____	1._____	1._____
2. _____	2._____	2._____
3. _____	3._____	3._____

_____

_____

_____

_____

_____

B. Product: Computer chips

CANADIAN AIR FORCE	EDMONTON POLICE DEPARTMENT	METRO TRANSIT
1._____	1._____	1._____
2._____	2._____	2._____
3._____	3._____	3._____

II.

"Researchers have identified as many as five specific roles that an individual in a buying center can play."

                          Users
                          Influencers
                          Buyers
                          Deciders
                          Gatekeepers

Match the correct "role" to the descriptions below:

1. _____These individuals have the formal authority and responsibility to select the supplier and negotiate the terms of the contract.

2. _____These people control the flow of information to other members of the buying center.

3. _____These people have the formal or informal power to select or approve the supplier that receives the contract.

4. _____These people affect the buying decision usually by helping define the specifications for what is bought.

5. _____These people in the organization actually use the product or service.

STAGES IN AN ORGANIZATIONAL BUYING DECISION

III.

Both consumer purchases and industrial purchases go through five distinct phases:

> Problem recognition
> Information search
> Alternative evaluation
> Purchase decision
> Postpurchase evaluation.

However, they differ in approach.

(A) Which of the following statements describe a <u>consumer purchase</u> and which describe an <u>industrial purchase</u>? (B) Identify the phase of the purchase process that is being described.

1.a. _____ A buying center uses price, delivery, and service, as
   b. _____ key criteria in considering new computer systems.
   They negotiate terms with a supplier and award a
   contract.

2.a. _____ A dentist asks his neighbor for the name of a
   b. _____ reputable electrician who can install home burglar
   alarms.

3.a. _____ A homeowner looks in the "Yellow Pages" for
   b. _____ professional lawn care services because he has no
   time to do the work himself.

4.a. _____ Suppliers are evaluated using a formal compensatory
   b. _____ vendor rating system. For example, prompt delivery
   is weighted most important at Acme Bearings, Inc.

5.a. _____ A clerk notices that the supply of legal-sized
   b. _____ envelopes will last three more days. He sends a
   requisition to the purchasing department.

6.a. _____ A professor visits several travel agencies to
   b. _____ investigate different European vacation package
   plans.

7.a. _____ A musician invites all his friends over to hear his
   b. _____ new sound system.

8.a. _____ A professional couple puts $5,000 down as earnest
   b. _____ money for an exclusive condominium.

9.a. _____ Before any decisions concerning the renovation of the
   b. _____ restaurant are made, the owners ask the cook,
   waitresses, hostess and busboys for suggestions.

10.a._____ A college professor asks several publishing companies
   b. _____ to send sample text books and she reviews them before
   deciding which marketing text to order for her
   classes.

5-7

BUY CLASSES

"Researchers who have studied organizational buying identify three types of buying situations which they have termed buy classes."

They are:
                Straight rebuy
                Modified rebuy
                New buy

Match the correct buying situation to the situations below.

1. _____ The buyer or purchasing manager reorders a ¼" ball bearing from the organization's list of ten acceptable suppliers on the bidders list.

2. _____ Eaton's is considering a line of food dehydrators and is approached by ABC Food Systems. Eaton's has never carried this type of product before.

3. _____ The owner of a small (but profitable) accounting firm looks into buying a small corporate jet.

4. _____ "Call Jake and tell him to send us three more cases of tomato paste."

5. _____ "Engineering has come up with a new design for the motor's cooling system that can save $20 per unit in assembly costs. I wonder if Ace Cooling Systems (our current supplier) can meet the tolerances for the new design."

6. _____ Extra-Strength Tylenol changes the design of its package to make it tamper-proof.

QUICK RECALL

I. What are three types of organizational markets?

1. _____

2. _____

3. _____

II. Name seven buying criteria commonly used by organizational buyers.

1. _____

2. _____

3. _____

4. _____

5. _____

6. _____

7. _____

III. What are five different roles in the buying center?

1. _____

2. _____

3. _____

4. _____

5. _____

IV. What are the five steps in an organizational buying decision process?

1. _____

2. _____

3. _____

4. _____

5. _____

V. Name the three buy classes.

1. _____

2. _____

3. _____

VI. What are four key lessons firms should learn when <u>selling</u> to organizations?

1. _____

2. _____

3. _____

4. _____

ANSWERS

TERMS AND DEFINITIONS

1. straight rebuy
2. value analysis
3. buying objectives
4. industrial firm
5. modified rebuy
6. buying center
7. make-buy decision
8. organizational buyer
9. buy classes
10. bidders list

11. government units
12. new buy
13. resellers
14. standard industrial classification (SIC) system
15. organizational buying behaviour
16. organizational buying criteria
17. reciprocity
18. derived demand

ORGANIZATIONAL BUYERS

1. government
2. industrial
3. industrial
4. industrial
5. resellers

6. industrial
7. government
8. industrial
9. government
10. industrial

MEASURING INDUSTRIAL, RESELLER, AND GOVERNMENT MARKETS

I. ADVANTAGES

1. Can be used to identify potential customers.
2. Can be used to monitor market opportunities and potential.

DISADVANTAGES

1. Classifications are only by major activity.
2. Not available for all industries in all geographic areas.

CHARACTERISTICS OF ORGANIZATIONAL BUYING

I. BUYING CRITERIA

A,B There are many possible correct answers. For further guidance refer to your text page(s): 124-126.

II. BUYING CENTERS

1. buyers
2. gatekeepers
3. deciders
4. influencers
5. users

III. STAGES IN AN ORGANIZATIONAL BUYING DECISION

1. industrial, purchase decision
2. consumer, information search
3. consumer, information search
4. industrial, alternative evaluation
5. industrial, problem recognition
6. consumer, alternative evaluation
7. consumer, postpurchase evaluation
8. consumer, purchase decision
9. industrial, information search
10. industrial, alternative evaluation

BUY CLASSES

1. straight rebuy
2. new buy
3. new buy
4. straight rebuy
5. modified rebuy
6. modified rebuy

QUICK RECALL

I. 1. industrial
    2. reseller
    3. government

II. 1. price
    2. ability to meet specifications
    3. delivery schedules
    4. technical ability
    5. warranties/Service
    6. past performance
    7. production capabilities

III. 1. user
     2. influencer
     3. gatekeeper
     4. buyer
     5. decider

IV. 1. problem recognition
    2. information search
    3. alternative evaluation
    4. purchase decision
    5. post-purchase evaluation

V. 1. new buy
    2. straight rebuy
    3. modified rebuy

VI. 1. Understand organizations' needs.
    2. Get on the right bidder's list.
    3. Reach the right people in the buying center.
    4. "Do the job."

6

COLLECTING MARKETING INFORMATION

Listed below are the definitions of important marketing terms. Choose the correct term for each definition from the list below, and write it in the space provided.

Alternatives
Assumptions
Constraints
Data
Decision
Decision factors
Dependent variable
Experimental independent variable
Experiments
Extraneous independent variable
Hypothesis
Marketing research
Measures of success

Methods
New product concept
Nonprobability sampling
Objectives
Observational data
Panel
Primary data
Probability sampling
Questionnaire data
Secondary data
Statistical inference
Uncertainties

1. _____The goals the decision maker seeks to achieve in solving a problem.

2. _____Criteria or standards used in evaluating proposed solutions to the problem.

3. _____Factors over which the decision maker has complete command.

4. _____A type of sampling that uses arbitrary judgments to select the sample so that the chance of selecting a particular element may be unknown or zero.

5. _____The restrictions placed on potential solutions by the nature and importance of the problems.

6. _____A method of drawing conclusions about a population based on information drawn from a sample of that population.

7. _____Data is obtained by manipulating factors under tightly controlled conditions to test cause and effect.

8. _____Precise rules are used to select the sample such that each element of the population has a specific known chance of being selected.

9. _____ Facts and figures which are new and are collected for the first time for the project at hand.

10. _____ Collected by watching either mechanically or in person how people actually behave.

11. _____ A data collection instrument used in mail surveys, telephone surveys, and personal interviews (see Figure 6-6 in text).

12. _____ The process of defining a marketing problem and then systematically collecting and analyzing information to recommend actions to improve an organization's marketing activities.

13. _____ Conjectures about factors or situations that simplify the problem enough to allow it to be solved within constraints.

14. _____ The sets of variables - the alternatives and uncertainties - that combine to give the outcome of a decision.

15. _____ Uncontrollable factors that the decision maker cannot influence.

16. _____ A tentative description of a product or service a firm might offer for sale.

17. _____ The approaches a researcher or decision maker can use to solve all or part of a problem.

18. _____ Facts and figures which have already been recorded.

19. _____ A conjecture about the relationship of two or more factors or what might happen in the future.

20. _____ A conscious choice from among two or more alternatives.

21. _____ The causal condition in an experiment; a factor that is expected to cause a change in the dependent variable.

22. _____ A sample of consumers or stores from which researchers take a series of periodic measurements.

23. _____ The factor of interest in an experiment that may be affected by the change in an independent variable.

24. _____ The facts, and figures pertinent to the problems composed of primary and secondary data.

25. _____ The causal condition due to factors that the experimenter cannot control but might change the behaviour of what is studied.

STEPS IN MAKING EFFECTIVE DECISIONS: DECIDE

"The systematic approach to making decisions (or problem solving)
. . . is based on six steps, represented by the acronym DECIDE."

I.   List the six steps in the DECIDE process:

    1. D._____
    2. E._____
    3. C._____
    4. I._____
    5. D._____
    6. E._____

II. List three major difficulties inherent in consumer research:

    1. _____

    _____

    2. _____

    _____

    3. _____

    _____

STEP 1 IN DECIDE: DEFINE THE PROBLEM

Step one in the decision making process (DECIDE) is to define the problem. Four factors must be considered:

> Objectives
> Constraints
> Assumptions
> Measures of success

Match the correct factor in the "Define" stage of the DECIDE process with the examples below.

I. 1. _____ Fisher-Price had to decide whether to market their original toy chatter phone or their new version toy chatter phone.

2. _____ Fisher-Price believed the children testing the toy phones were typical of all children in their target market.

3. _____ The amount of time the children spent playing with the toy phones would be the influencing factor on the final marketing action. The children spent more time playing with the new design.

4. _____ Fisher-Price had only ten weeks to make a decision on the toy chatter phone.

II. 1. _____ A new restaurant only has enough money budgeted to advertise monthly in one of four major publications. They need to find which publication will give them the best return on their advertising investment.

2. _____ The restaurant places a small coupon ad in each newspaper simultaneously. Each coupon is coded. The restaurant owner feels that the newspaper with the most redeemed coupons is the best newspaper in which to place the ad.

3. _____ Prices for advertising are scheduled to go up in all four newspapers on June 1st, only two weeks away.

4. _____ In order for any of the ads to be profitable a minimum of 125 coupons must be redeemed.

STEP 2 IN DECIDE: ENUMERATE THE DECISION FACTORS

I. **Alternatives: The controllable decision factors**

"Experienced marketing managers insist on searching for more than a single alternative solution to a problem because the new alternatives may lead to better solutions."

One way to do this is to start the problem with the statement, "In what ways can we . . ."

Given that you are the marketing manager for a firm that manufactures cotton swabs, list at least six "In what ways . . ." statements.

1. _____

2. _____

3. _____

4. _____

5. _____

6. _____

II. Uncertainties

"Uncertainties are the uncontrollable factors that the decision maker cannot influence."

*Challenge - "uncertainties." Make a list of as many other product failure examples you can find. Be sure to list both the product and reason for failure.

Example:
edible bubble gum	technology	safe foaming agents didn't make good bubbles
_____	_____	_____
_____	_____	_____
_____	_____	_____
_____	_____	_____
_____	_____	_____

STEP 3 IN DECIDE: COLLECT RELEVANT INFORMATION

"Marketing researchers often select a group of customers or prospects, ask them questions, and treat their answers as typical of all those in whom they are interested."

Sampling has two variations:

> Probability
> Nonprobability

Decide whether the following statements are examples of probability or nonprobability sampling.

1. _____ A doctoral student requests access to a list of magazine subscribers whose last names all begin with the letter "M." He wants to study the effect of sex appeal in advertising for his thesis.

2. _____ A junior high principal wants to study the use of alcohol by his students. He selects one hundred students by choosing every tenth name on his enrollment list.

3. _____ A principal at the junior high across town wants to attempt the same study as the principal in the previous question, but he chooses the one hundred students with the lowest grade point average.

4. _____ A public transit authority manager wants to collect data in order to make decisions concerning new bus routes. He surveys every 5th person who board buses in the area affected by the proposed route changes.

SECONDARY DATA

Good decision making depends a great deal upon good data collection.

"Secondary data are those facts which have already been recorded."

Secondary data can be internal - information which exists inside the business firm, or external - which is data published outside the firm.

I.   Make a list of at least five important external secondary data sources.

1.   _____

2.   _____

3.   _____

4.   _____

5.   _____

*Challenge - Try to locate these sources in different libraries. Familiarize yourself with the different publications' formats.

II. Secondary data has both advantages and disadvantages.

Read the following statements concerning secondary data and decide if they are advantages or disadvantages.

1.   _____Secondary data is dated material.

2.   _____Secondary data is time efficient.

3.   _____The format of secondary data is determined by the collecting agency.

4.   _____Secondary data is inexpensive to obtain.

OBSERVATIONAL DATA

There are two major ways to obtain primary data: by observing people and by asking them questions.

Observational data can be collected either mechanically or in person.

I.   List 4 advantages of the observational method of data collection.

1._____

2._____

3._____

4._____

II. List 4 disadvantages of the observational method of data collection.

5._____

6._____

7._____

8._____

QUESTIONNAIRE

"Many marketing researchers distinguish questionnaire data used for hypothesis generation from that used for hypothesis evaluation."

I.   List two possible methods of obtaining questionnaire data for hypothesis generation.

1._____

2._____

"In hypothesis evaluation the marketing researcher tests ideas discovered in the idea generation stage to help the marketing manager recommend marketing actions."

II. What is the biggest factor a marketing manager must consider when choosing between the three forms of questionnaires?

_____

QUESTIONNAIRE DATA

There are several types of questions which may appear on a questionnaire.

        Open-ended
        Fixed Alternative
        Fixed Alternative - Dichotomous Scale
        Fixed Alternative - Semantic Differential
        Fixed Alternative - Likert Scale

I.   Match the type of question to the examples below:

    1. _____ [] Male, [] Female

    2. _____ [] Mr., [] Mrs., [] Ms., [] Miss

    3. _____ What is your attitude toward sweetened cereals?

    4. _____ My professor's tests are:

Very Difficult   ____ ____ ____ ____ ____   Very Easy

Too Long   ____ ____ ____ ____ ____   Too Short

    5. _____ Children should be seen and not heard . . .

        Strongly   Don't   Strongly
        Agree   Agree   Know   Disagree   Disagree
         []   []   []   []   []

    6. _____The reason I took this course is . . .

II. Questions designed for your data collection on questionnaires must not be biased.

    Below are poorly constructed questions. Rewrite each question to get the most accurate data.

1. Do you exercise often?

    _____

2. Do you prefer the sadistic inhumane neutering of loving family pets or the benevolent construction of pet care shelters?

    _____

3. Whom do you live with? [] Parents, [] Spouse

    _____

4. Do you read mysteries and science fiction? [] Yes, [] No

_____

5. My weight is between: [] 100-120 lbs., [] 120-140 lbs., [] 140-160 lbs.
                           [] over 160 lbs.

_____

6. How many students in your class ate breakfast last Monday?

_____

EXPERIMENTS

"Two ways that observations and questionnaires are used are in experiments and panels."

"Experiments manipulate a situation to measure the effect of an independent variable (cause) on the dependent variable (result or effect)."

Identify the independent variable(s), dependent variable(s), and any extraneous variable(s) in the experiment below:

A grocery store manager set up a display of canned green beans at the end of an aisle and placed a large sign there that said "green beans 3/$1.25." On the shelf, half way down the aisle in their regular location, the identical green beans were being sold for 40¢ apiece. The store manager wanted to see if people would buy things marked in quantity rather than things marked individually, regardless of price.

*Challenge - Discuss the problems in this experiment and decide how you would change it while still seeking the same information.

_____

_____

_____

QUICK RECALL

I. List four key elements used to define a problem.

   1. _____

   2. _____

   3. _____

   4. _____

II. List the six steps in the acronym DECIDE.

   1. _____

   2. _____

   3. _____

   4. _____

   5. _____

   6. _____

III. What are the two types of sampling?

   1. _____

   2. _____

IV. Information collected can be classified in three ways:

   1. _____

   2. _____

   3. _____

V. What are five types of questions which may appear on a questionnaire?

   1. _____

   2. _____

   3. _____

   4. _____

   5. _____

TERMS AND DEFINITIONS

1. objectives
2. measures of success
3. alternatives
4. nonprobability sampling
5. constraints
6. statistical inference
7. experiment
8. probability sampling
9. primary data
10. observational data
11. questionnaire
12. marketing research
13. assumptions
14. decision factors
15. uncertainties
16. new product concept
17. methods
18. secondary data
19. hypothesis
20. decision
21. independent variable
22. panel
23. dependent variable
24. data
25. extraneous independent variable

STEPS IN MAKING EFFECTIVE DECISIONS: DECIDE

I.
1. Define the problem
2. Enumerate the decision factors
3. Collect relevant information
4. Identify a solution
5. Develop and implement a plan
6. Evaluate the results

II.
1. Do consumers really know they will buy a product they have never thought about before?
2. Even if they know the answer, will they reveal it?
3. Will their actual purchase behaviour be the same as their stated intentions?

STEP 1 IN DECIDE: DEFINE THE PROBLEM

I.
1. objectives
2. assumptions
3. measures of success
4. constraints

II.
1. objectives
2. assumptions
3. constraints
4. measures of success

STEP 2 IN DECIDE: ENUMERATE THE DECISION FACTORS

I.   In what ways . . .
           can we put cotton swabs to new use?
           can we reach new markets?
           can we better distribute the product to the customer?
           can we convince more dealers to carry our product?
           can we convince consumers of the benefits of using our brand?

II. There are many possible correct answers. For further guidance refer to
    your text pages: 150.

STEP 3 IN DECIDE: COLLECT RELEVANT INFORMATION

1. nonprobability   3. nonprobability
2. probability   4. nonprobability

SECONDARY DATA

     Numerous possible answers (check Chapter 6).

I.   1. Census of Canada
      2. Market Research Handbook
      3. The Census of Manufacturers
      4. Sales and Marketing Management Magazine
      5. Canadian Markets

II. 1. disadvantage   3. disadvantage
    2. advantage   4. advantage

OBSERVATIONAL DATA

I & II

     Several of the answers to this question are found within the chapter.
There are numerous correct answers available from outside sources as well.

QUESTIONNAIRE

I.   1. personal (individual) interviews
     2. focus groups

II. The marketing manager must balance cost against expected quality of
    information obtained.

QUESTIONNAIRE DATA

I. 1. fixed alternative - dichotomous scale
    2. fixed alternative
    3. open-ended
    4. fixed alternative - semantic differential
    5. likert
    6. open-ended

II. Check your answers against Figure 6-7 in your text to make sure you didn't repeat any mistakes.

EXPERIMENTS

dependent variable - sales
independent variable - price/quantity
extraneous variables - (many possible) signing, location, etc.

(Remember, this was an example of a poor experiment. In a good experiment all variables should be clearly defined.)

QUICK RECALL

I. 1. objectives
    2. constraints
    3. assumptions
    4. measures of success

II. 1. define the problem
    2. enumerate the decision factors

    3. collect relevant information

    4. identify a solution
    5. develop and implement a plan
    6. evaluate the results

III. 1. probability
     2. nonprobability

IV. 1. ideas
    2. methods
    3. data

V. 1. open-ended
    2. fixed alternative
    3. dichotomous
    4. semantic differential
    5. Likert scale

7

ANALYZING MARKETING INFORMATION AND MAKING FORECASTS

Listed below are the definitions of important marketing terms. Choose the correct term for each definition from the list below, and write it in the space provided.

Buildup approach
Delphi method
Direct forecast
Field experiments
Jury of executive opinion
Laboratory experiment
Lost-horse forecasting
Market potential (industry potential)
Marketing Decision Support System MDSS
Sales force survey

Sales forecast (company forecast)
Sensitivity analysis
Solution
Survey of buyers' intentions
Survey of experts
Technological forecasting
Top-down approach
Trend extrapolation

1. _____ The best alternative that has been identified.

2. _____ A method by which people knowledgeable about a forecast topic are polled.

3. _____ The maximum total sales of a product by all firms to a segment under specified environmental conditions and marketing efforts of the firms.

4. _____ Analyzing how making slight changes in factors like price or advertising levels affect sales revenue or other results of marketing programs.

5. _____ Simulating some market-related activity in a highly controlled setting.

6. _____ What one firm expects to sell under the specified conditions for the uncontrollable and controllable factors that affect the forecast.

7. _____ Extending a pattern observed in past data into the future.

8. _____ A computerized method of providing timely, accurate information to improve making decisions.

9. _____ Estimating when scientific breakthroughs will occur so the firm can prepare for them.

10. _____ Involves subdividing an aggregate estimate into its principal components.

11. _____ A sales forecasting technique that sums the sales forecasts of each of the components to arrive at a total forecast.

12. _____ A test of some marketing variables in actual store or buying settings.

13. _____ A survey of knowledgeable executives inside a firm and a combination of their opinions to obtain a sales forecast.

14. _____ A survey in which a group of experts gives anonymous forecasts of sales or of the probability of some future event; estimates are summarized and reported back to them, and they may revise them for several rounds.

15. _____ Asking prospective customers whether they are likely to buy the product or service during some future time period.

16. _____ Estimates by a firm's salespeople of sales during a coming period.

17. _____ An estimate of the value to be forecast without the use of intervening steps.

18. _____ Forecasting by starting with the last known value of an item, identifying positive and negative factors that might affect it, and estimating where it might end up.

STEP 4 IN DECIDE: IDENTIFY THE BEST ALTERNATIVE

Use the information you learned in Chapter 7, along with any information you have acquired in previous chapters to answer the following questions: Be as thorough as possible.

You are the marketing manager of a fast food hamburger franchise. You are considering opening 100 of your stores for business at 7:00 a.m. in order to attract the breakfast trade. There are a number of decisions which must be made.

You begin with the following quantifiable <u>measures of success</u>:

1. If during a trial week period breakfast sales are less than $500, discontinue project.

2. If during a trial week period breakfast sales are between $550 and $750, continue project temporarily, while exploring possible methods of increasing sales.

3. If sales exceed $750, open for breakfast on a permanent basis.

I.   If during a one-week period average breakfast sales are $610.00, what is your next course of action?

_____

_____

*Challenge - Four stores were tested, each in a different geographic region. Breakfast sales at three stores averaged $600.00, but sales at the fourth store were only $400.00. What would you do?

II. For the following situations, design a laboratory experiment that will help identify which three breakfast items should be served.

    Based upon a four-state test, you decide there is a sufficient potential market for a breakfast operation. You must now decide what to serve. For maximum efficiency you want to serve only three main breakfast items. The following items can be prepared with little or no additional costs other than ingredients: omelets, egg sandwiches, pancakes, french toast, or fruit muffins. The products were equal in dollar return during the test.

_____

_____

_____

III. For the following scenario, design a quantifiable measure of success using $1200 as your minimum acceptable sales volume.

    On the basis of the experimental data you collected, you decide to serve omelets, pancakes, and egg sandwiches. After opening for business you still need to increase your sales in order to make the breakfast business permanent.

    A number of store managers comment that customers are asking for waffles for breakfast. You decide that it may be profitable to invest in the equipment to make waffles (something your competition has not done).

_____

_____

_____

IV. Design a field experiment using two stores to determine if serving waffles is a viable alternative.

_____

_____

_____

_____

_____

STEP 5 IN DECIDE: DESIGN AND IMPLEMENT
A DETAILED PLAN

Using the information in the previous exercise, in addition to any (imaginary) information you may have collected as marketing manager, proceed with step 5 of the DECIDE process.

List at least 7 specific steps for your marketing plan.

_____

_____

_____

_____

_____

_____

_____

STEP 6 IN DECIDE: EVALUATE THE RESULTS

Step 6 in the DECIDE process is, "evaluate the results."

List the two important elements which must be evaluated:

_____

_____

MARKETING DECISION SUPPORT SYSTEMS (MDSS)

"A marketing decision support system is a computerized method of providing timely, accurate information to improve marketing decisions."

There are four basic elements found in an MDSS today. Match the correct term with the definitions listed below:

> Data bank
> Links
> Models
> System interrogation

1. _____A means of tying the data banks to the models.

2. _____A means of communicating with the entire system so the manager can ask questions and get answers quickly (A reason for direct access to the system through a terminal or personal computer on the manager's desk).

3. _____Ideas or hypotheses about the relationships between the factors a marketing manager controls and the results sought.

4. _____A collection of libraries of information. In marketing, these might include sales by type of outlet and geographic area, as well as customer data reported by the sales force resulting from sales calls.

WHEN AN MDSS IS NEEDED

"A sales manager makes two distinctly different kinds of decisions: repetitive and nonrepetitive."

Which of the following statements reflect nonrepetitive decisions and which statements reflect repetitive decisions?

1. _____Whether to change the location of a branch bank from Halifax to Dartmouth.

2. _____Whether to increase the advertising budget preceding holiday weekends.

3. _____Whether to test market product X in Vancouver or Toronto.

4. _____How to allocate personnel to sales territories.

BASIC FORECASTING TERMS

Match the following terms to the examples below:

Lost horse
Direct forecast
Survey of buyer's intentions
Jury of executive opinion
Sales force survey
Delphi method
Technological forecasting
Trend extrapolation

1. _____How many days ahead should I buy the party invitations?

2. _____At the end of swimming lessons the class is asked how many students think they will enroll for the second session.

3. _____The vice presidents of marketing, research and development, finance, and production at Apple Computer met for a two-day conference to discuss and propose the forecast projections for the following year.

4. _____A computer expert explains that within five years computerizing truck dispatch will reduce personnel, increase efficiency, and significantly reduce costs.

5. _____Three different people, all well-known figures in their field, submit anonymous forecasts for a certain industry's projected growth. All three read each other's forecasts and rationale. The process is then repeated to ensure the most accurate appraisal.

6. _____All salespeople who have been involved with a company's product are asked to give forecasts based upon both their actual sales experience and personal impressions of a given product.

7. _____Sales forecasts are based on data accumulated over a number of years. It is assumed that sales will continue to grow in the future at the same rate as in the past.

8. _____A video game manufacturer uses the sales information from last year, plus the number of new games being developed, plus the number of video parlors that have closed in the past year, in addition to a number of other factors when figuring the forecast for next year.

TWO BASIC APPROACHES TO FORECASTING

"The two basic approaches to sales forecasting are (1) subdividing the total sales forecast (top-down approach) or (2) building the total sales forecast by summing the components (buildup approach)."

1a. Use the Buying Power Index (BPI) to figure the sales percentage for the province of Ontario given the following information:

BPI= (0.2 x percent of population)+(0.5 x percent of Personal Income)+(0.3 x percent of retail sales)

Percent of population   = 36.4
Percent of National Personal Income = 42.3
Percent of retail sales   = 38.5

BPI = _____

1b. If an appliance manufacture estimates total market potential for microwave ovens in 1992 to be 2 million units, what would the sales potential be for Ontario (using the BPI alone)? _____

2. Use the buildup approach to forecast company sales based on the information given below:

	Units
Atlantic Provinces manager's regional forecast	28,000
Quebec manager's regional forecast	24,500
Ontario manager's regional forecast	21,700
Western manager's regional forecast	19,700
B.C. manager's regional forecast	29,900

Company forecast: _____ units

SPECIFIC SALES FORECASTING TECHNIQUES

There are four specific sales forecasting techniques:

Judgments of decision maker
Surveys of knowledgeable groups
Statistical methods

Listed below are methods of sales forecasting which are examples of the types of techniques listed above.

I.   Match the following methods to the correct sales forecasting technique.

1. _____Sales force survey

2. _____Lost horse

3. _____Linear trend extrapolation

4. _____Direct forecast

5. _____Technological forecasting

6. _____Survey of buyer's intentions

7. _____Trend extrapolation

8. _____Delphi method

9. _____Jury of executive opinion

II. Which of the four techniques is most commonly used?

1. _____

QUICK RECALL

I.   What are the six steps in the DECIDE process?

1._____

2._____

3._____

4._____

5._____

6._____

II. What are two commonly used methods of experimentation?

1._____

2._____

III. What are the two key factors that should be evaluated in step 6 of DECIDE?

1._____

2._____

IV. What are four key elements of an MDSS?

1._____

2._____

3._____

4._____

V. What are two types of decisions a marketing manager makes?

1._____   2._____

VI. What are the two basic approaches to forecasting?

1._____

2._____

VII. List the three specific sales forecasting techniques.

1._____

2._____

3._____

VIII. List two examples of a "judgment of individuals" forecasting technique.

1._____

2._____

IX. List six examples of a "survey of knowledgeable groups" forecasting technique.

1._____

2._____

3._____

4._____

5._____

6._____

X. List two examples of a "statistical method" of forecasting.

1._____

2._____

TERMS AND DEFINITIONS

1. solution
2. survey of experts
3. market potential (industry potential)
4. sensitivity analysis
5. laboratory experiment
6. sales forecast (company forecast)
7. trend extrapolation
8. MDSS
9. technological forecasting
10. top-down approach
11. buildup approach
12. field experiment
13. jury of executive opinion
14. delphi method
15. survey of buyers' intention
16. sales force survey
17. direct forecast
18. lost-horse forecasting

STEP 4 IN DECIDE: IDENTIFY THE BEST ALTERNATIVE

I.   According to your measures of success you should continue the project temporarily while exploring additional methods of increasing sales.

II. There are an infinite number of ways to design your experiment. However, be sure you identify any or all dependent, independent, and extraneous variables before you begin. Compare answers with a friend to be sure there are no hidden factors.

III. Example: ($1200 - Cost) $\geq$ $200

IV. Follow the same procedure as in answer II.

STEPS 5 IN DECIDE: DESIGN AND IMPLEMENT A DETAILED PLAN

There are many possible correct answers. For further guidance refer to your text page(s): 179-180. Be sure your answer addresses aspects of all four P's. For example, if you are going to advertise your new hours, which mediums will you use? Be specific.

STEP 6 IN DECIDE: EVALUATE THE RESULTS

1. Evaluate the decision itself
2. Evaluate the decision process

MARKETING DECISION SUPPORT SYSTEMS

1. links
2. system interrogation
3. models
4. data bank

WHEN AN MDSS IS NEEDED

1. nonrepetitive
2. repetitive
3. nonrepetitive
4. repetitive

BASIC FORECASTING TERMS

1. direct forecast
2. survey of buyer's intentions
3. jury of executive opinion
4. technological forecasting

5. delphi method
6. sales force survey
7. trend extrapolation
8. lost horse

TWO BASIC APPROACHES TO FORECASTING

1a.   B.P.I = 39.98 percent
1b.   800,000 microwaves
2.   123,800 units

SPECIFIC SALES FORECASTING TECHNIQUES

I. 1. surveys of knowledgeable
       groups
    2. judgments of decision maker
    3. statistical methods
    4. judgments of decision maker
    5. survey of knowledgeable
       groups

    6. surveys of knowledgeable
       groups
    7. statistical methods
    8. survey of knowledgeable
       groups
    9. survey of knowledgeable
       groups

II. Judgments of individuals

QUICK RECALL

I.   1. Define the problem
      2. Enumerate the decision factors
      3. Collect the relevant information
      4. Identify the solution
      5. Develop and implement a plan
      6. Evaluate the results

II.   1. laboratory experiments
      2. field experiments

III. 1. evaluate the results
      2. evaluate the decision process

IV.   1. data banks
      2. models
      3. links
      4. systems interrogation

V.   1. repetitive decisions
      2. nonrepetitive decisions

VI.   1. top-down
      2. buildup

VII. 1. judgments of the decision-maker
2. surveys of knowledgeable groups
3. statistical methods

VIII. 1. direct forecast
2. lost-horse

IX. 1. survey of buyers' intentions
2. sales force survey
3. jury of executive opinion
4. Delphi method
5. survey of experts
6. technological forecasting

X. 1. trend extrapolation
2. linear trend extrapolation

8

MARKET SEGMENTATION, TARGETING, AND POSITIONING

TERMS AND DEFINITIONS

Listed below are the definitions of important marketing terms. Choose the correct term for each definition from the list below, and write it in the space provided.

Cross tabulation
Market segmentation
Market segments
Market-product grid
Perceptual map
Product differentiation

Product positioning
Prospect
Psychographic variables
Repositioning
Usage rate
80/20 rule

1. _____ Aggregating prospective buyers into groups that 1) have common needs, and 2) will respond similarly to a marketing action.

2. _____ Relatively homogeneous collections of prospective buyers.

3. _____ A framework to relate the segments of a market to products offered or potential marketing actions by the firm.

4. _____ Involves a firm selling two or more products with different features targeted to different market segments.

5. _____ Consumer activities, interests, and opinions.

6. _____ The quantity consumed or patronage (store visits) during a specific period which varies significantly among different customer groups.

7. _____ A rule which suggests that eighty percent of a firm's sales are obtained from twenty percent of its customers.

8. _____ A method of presenting and relating data having two or more variables. It is used to analyze and discover relationships in the data.

9. _____ The place an offering occupies in consumer's minds on important attributes relative to competing offerings.

10. _____ A display or graph in two dimensions locating products or brands in the minds of consumers.

11. _____ Changing a product's or brand's image in consumers' minds.

WHY SEGMENT MARKETS?

"Market segmentation is dividing a market into distinct groups that (1) have common needs, and (2) will respond similarly to a marketing action."

I.   Segment the markets for the following products into four market segments.

A. Shampoo

1. _____

2. _____

3. _____

4. _____

B. Bicycles

1. _____

2. _____

3. _____

4. _____

C. Laundry and Dry Cleaning Services

1. _____

2. _____

3. _____

4. _____

II. What are the advantages and disadvantages of using:
1. single product/multiple market
2. multiple product/multiple market segmentation?

SINGLE PRODUCT/MULTIPLE MARKET

Advantages

1. _____

2. _____

Disadvantages

1. _____

2. _____

MULTIPLE PRODUCT/MULTIPLE MARKET

Advantages   Disadvantages

1. _____   1. _____

2. _____   2. _____

III. CRITERIA USED IN FORMING MARKET SEGMENTS

There are five principal criteria used when forming segments in a market:

Potential for increased profit.
Similarity of needs of potential buyers within a segment.
Difference of needs of buyers between segments.
Feasibility of a marketing action to reach a segment.
Simplicity and cost of assigning potential buyers to a segment.

Using the Reebok example from your text, give a concrete illustration for each of the criteria listed above.

1. _____

_____

2. _____

_____

3 _____

_____

4. _____

_____

5. _____

_____

WAYS TO SEGMENT CONSUMER MARKETS

Variables that can be used to segment consumer markets can be divided into two main categories:

Customer characteristics
Buying situations

Which of the following statements below are examples of customer characteristics, and which are examples of buying situations?

1. _____Chrysler found that pickup trucks are widely used in Atlantic Canada and Western Canada. Because many pickup truck drivers listen to country and western music, Chrysler advertises on C & W radio stations in this region.

2. _____Del Monte now promotes a line of canned fruits and vegetables that have low salt and low sugar.

3. _____Because well-known celebrities can't shop in peace due to "fan adoration," several mail order catalogues carry very exclusive, very expensive merchandise.

4. _____Because smaller households often have smaller kitchens, General Electric downsized its microwave oven.

5. _____A national beer company targets 60 percent of its advertising dollars to people who buy at least a case of beer per week.

WAYS TO SEGMENT INDUSTRIAL MARKETS

There are four main dimensions when choosing variables to segment an industrial market:

Customer Characteristics
1. Geographic
2. Demographic

Buying Situation
1. Nature of the good
2. Buying condition

Using Figure 8-7 in the text as a guideline, select one variable from each main dimension and give a concrete example for it, then try to think of a product or service for which you might use this type of segmentation, for example:

Main Dimension	Variable	Example	Product/Service
Geographic	a. region	b. Ontario	c. Industrial Screws
1. Geographic	a. _____	b. _____	c. _____
2. Demographic	a. _____	b. _____	c. _____
3. Nature of good	a. _____	b. _____	c. _____
4. Buying condition	a. _____	b. _____	c. _____

GROUPING PRODUCTS TO BE SOLD

I. "As important as grouping customers into segments is finding a means of grouping the products you're selling into meaningful categories."

Below is a list of twenty items sold by a single company. Group these products into meaningful categories. List both the criteria used and the items included.

Permanent markers
Rulers
Protractors
Pencils
Colored chalk
Compasses
Letter openers
Crayons
Paper clips
Tape

Glue
Pocket dictionaries
Pocket atlases
Erasers
Thesauruses
Thumb tacks
Paperweights
Staples
Rubber bands
Ballpoint pens

Criteria	Item(s)

*Example:
    Metal items

Compasses, letter openers, paper clips, thumb tacks, staples.

1. _____   _____

2. _____   _____

3. _____   _____

4. _____   _____

*There may be more appropriate groupings for these items.

II. Select targets on which to focus efforts.

In addition to the five criteria used for dividing the market into segments, there are five different criteria for selecting the target market segments that will be the focus of your marketing plan. They are:

> Size
> Expected growth
> Competitive position
> Cost of reaching the segment
> Compatibility with the organization's objectives
> and resources

Using the example in Chapter 8 of a fast food hamburger restaurant, make statements (true or hypothetical) to illustrate each of the five criteria above.

1. _____

2. _____

3. _____

4. _____

5. _____

ANALYZING MARKET SEGMENTS USING CROSS TABULATION

"Cross tabulation or cross-tabs, is a method of presenting and relating information having two or more variables to display summary data and discover relationships in the data."

AGE OF HEAD OF HOUSEHOLD (YEARS)	FREQUENCY			
	ONCE A WEEK OR MORE	2 OR 3 TIMES A MONTH	ONCE A MONTH OR LESS	TOTAL
24 or less	144	52	19	215
25 to 39	46	58	29	133
40 or over	82	69	87	238
TOTAL	272	179	135	586

A

AGE OF HEAD OF HOUSEHOLD (YEARS)	FREQUENCY			
	ONCE A WEEK OR MORE	2 OR 3 TIMES A MONTH	ONCE A MONTH OR LESS	TOTAL
24 or less	67.0%	24.2%	8.8%	100.0%
25 to 39	34.6	43.6	21.8	100.0
40 or over	34.4	29.0	36.6	100.0
TOTAL	46.4%	30.6%	23.0%	100.0%

B

I. Using the cross tabulations above, answer the following questions.

1. _____ Which cross tabulation grid lists absolute frequencies?

2. _____ Which cross tabulation grid lists show percentages?

3. _____ Which age group eats fast foods most frequently?

4. _____ Less than 25 percent of which age group(s) eats out 2 or 3 times a month?

5. _____ What percentage of the total group sampled eats out once a week or more?

6. _____ Between which two groups is there the least percentage difference in the number of people eating out at any given frequency?

II. Which questions would you ask (i.e., which variables would you use) to find information about the clientele and usage of health spa facilities? List at least five.

1. _____

2. _____

3. _____

4. _____

5. _____

PRODUCT POSITIONING

There are two major approaches to product positioning:

    Head-to-Head - Competing directly with competitors on similar
             product attributes in the same target market.

    Differentiation - Seeking a smaller market niche that is less
             competitive in which to locate a brand.

Using television, radio, or print advertisements, make a list of five current
product campaigns using head-to-head positioning, and five current product
campaigns using product differentiation.

1. _____   1. _____

2. _____   2. _____

3. _____   3. _____

4. _____   4. _____

5. _____   5. _____

QUICK RECALL

I.   What are the two possible conditions you must consider when deciding
how to segment a market?

    1. _____

    2. _____

II.   What are the five criteria used when forming market segments?

    1. _____

    2. _____

    3. _____

    4. _____

    5. _____

III.   What are two ways to segment consumer markets?

    1. _____

    2. _____

IV.   What are four ways to segment an industrial market?

        1. _____

        2. _____

        3. _____

        4. _____

V.   What are five criteria used to select target segments?

        1. _____

        2. _____

        3. _____

        4. _____

        5. _____

VI.   What are two approaches to product positioning?

        1. _____

        2. _____

TERMS AND DEFINITIONS

1. market segmentation
2. market segment
3. market-product grid
4. product differentiation
5. psychographics
6. usage rate
7. 80/20 rule

8. cross tabulation
9. product positioning
10. perceptual map
11. repositioning

WHY SEGMENT MARKETS

There are many possible correct answers. For further guidance refer to text page(s): 200-201.

I. A.   babies, teens, adults, people with medicinal needs
    B.   children, teens, adult casual riders, adult serious riders
    C.   businesses with less than 100 employees, businesses with more than 100 employees, households-single, households-senior citizens.

II. Single Product/Multiple Market

Possible advantages:
1. avoid cost of new product development
2. lower manufacturing costs

Possible disadvantages:
1. may not be able to attract consumers
2. missed expansion opportunities

Multiple Product/Multiple Market

Possible advantages:
1. greater potential for higher profits & sales
2. can satisfy more consumers, build good will

Possible disadvantages:
1. higher manufacturing and promotion costs
2. costs of research and development

III. There are many possible correct answers. For further guidance refer to your text page(s): 202-204.

WAYS TO SEGMENT CONSUMER MARKETS

1. customer characteristics
2. buying situations
3. customer characteristics

4. customer characteristics
5. buying situations

WAYS TO SEGMENT INDUSTRIAL MARKETS

There are many possible correct answers. For further guidance refer to your text page(s): 210. Also, use Figure 8-7 as a guideline.

GROUPING PRODUCTS TO BE SOLD

I. There are many possible correct answers.
    1. Fasteners   3. Plastic/metal/paper items
    2. Writing instruments 4. books

II. There are many possible correct answers. For further guidance refer to your text page(s): 212-213.

ANALYZING MARKET SEGMENTS USING CROSS TABULATION

I.   1. A
     2. B
     3. 24 or less

4. 24 years or less
5. 46.4 percent
6. 25-39 -- 40 or over

II. There are many possible correct answers. For further guidance refer to your text page(s): 217.

PRODUCT POSITIONING

There are many possible correct answers. For further guidance refer to your text page(s): 219-220.

QUICK RECALL

I.   1. single product/multiple market
       2. multiple product/multiple market

II.   1. potential for increased profit
      2. similarity of needs of potential buyers within a segment
      3. difference of needs of buyers between segments
      4. feasibility of marketing action to reach a segment
      5. simplicity and cost of assigning potential buyers to a segment

III.   1. customer characteristics
      2. buying situations

IV.   1. geographic
      2. demographic

3. nature of goods
4. buying condition

V.   1. size
2. expected growth
3. competitive position
4. cost of reaching the segment
5. compatibility with the organization's objectives and resources

VI.   1. head-to-head
2. product differentiation

9

DEVELOPING NEW PRODUCTS

TERMS AND DEFINITIONS

Listed below are the definitions of important marketing terms. Choose the correct term for each definition from the list below, and write it in the space provided.

Business analysis
Commercialization
Consumer goods
Convenience goods
Development
Idea generation
Industrial goods
Market testing
New product process
New product strategy development
Proactive strategy

Product
Product line
Product mix
Production goods
Reactive strategy
Screening and evaluation
Shopping goods
Specialty goods
Support goods
Unsought goods

1. _____ A good, service, or idea consisting of a bundle of tangible and intangible attributes that satisfies customers and is received in exchange for money or another unit of value.

2. _____ The number of product lines offered by a company.

3. _____ Items that the consumer purchases frequently, conveniently, and with a minimum of shopping effort.

4. _____ A group of products that are closely related because they satisfy a class of needs, are used together, are sold to the same customer group, are distributed through the same type of outlets, and/or fall within a given price range.

5. _____ Products purchased by the ultimate consumer.

6. _____ Products for which the consumer will compare several alternatives on various criteria such as price, quality, or style.

7. _____ Seven steps taken in the commercialization of a new product: new product strategy, idea generation, screening and evaluation, business analysis, development, testing, and commercialization.

8. _____ Step one of the new product process, in which a firm defines the role for new products in terms of its overall corporate objectives.

9. _____ Step six in the new product process involves exposing actual products to prospective consumers under realistic purchase conditions to see if they will buy.

10. _____ Products used in the production of other products for ultimate consumers.

11. _____ Products used in the manufacturing of other items which become part of the final product.

12. _____ Those products for which a consumer will make a special effort to search out and buy.

13. _____ Items used to assist in the production of other goods.

14. _____ Step two of the new product process, in which a firm develops a pool of concepts as candidates for new products.

15. _____ Step four of the new product process, involves specifying product features and marketing strategy and making the financial projections needed to commercialize the product.

16. _____ Step five of the new product process, in which the idea-on-paper is turned into prototype, a demonstrable, producible product in hand.

17. _____ Step three of the new product process, in which a firm uses internal and external evaluations to eliminate ideas that warrant no further development effort.

18. _____ Step seven of the new product process, in which the product is positioned and launched into full-scale production and sale.

19. _____ Products which the consumer either does not know about or knows about, but does not initially want.

20. _____ A strategy leading to the allocation of resource to identify and seize opportunities.

21. _____ New product strategies that involve developing new products in response to competitors' new items. (taking a defensive approach).

PRODUCT LINE AND PRODUCT MIX

"A product is a good, service, or idea, consisting of a bundle of tangible and intangible attributes which satisfies consumers and is received in exchange for money or other units of value."

There are several important terms pertaining to variations of product:

Product line
Product item
Stock keeping unit
Product mix

Match the correct term to the statements below:

1. _____ The number of product lines a company carries.

2. _____ A group of products that are closely related because they satisfy a class of needs, are used together, are sold to the same customer group, are distributed through the same type of outlets, or fall within a given price range.

3. _____ A specific product as noted by a unique brand, size, or price.

4. _____ A distinct ordering code designated to each size of a given product.

CLASSIFYING PRODUCTS

"Two major ways to classify products are by degree of tangibility and by the type of user."

I. Classification by tangibility divides products into three groups:

Nondurable goods - Items consumed in one or a few uses.

Durable goods - Items that usually last over an extended number of uses.

Services - Activities, benefits, or satisfactions offered for sale.

Classify the following products listed below:

1. _____ Ketchup   4. _____ Paper plates

2. _____ Lawn care   5. _____ Day care

3. _____ Bath towels   6. _____ Carpeting

II. The second major type of product classification is based on the user.

Consumer goods - Products purchased by the ultimate consumer.

Industrial goods - Products used in the production of other products for ultimate consumers.

Classify the following products according to user:

1. _____Nails

2. _____Ball bearings

3. _____Printing press

4. _____Cake mix

5. _____Farm machinery

6. _____Suitcase

You may have had difficulty with the question above. Example: nails, cake mixes.

*Challenge - A problem with user classification is that some products can be considered both consumer and industrial goods. Make a list of ten commonly known products that may fall into this crossover category.

CONSUMER GOODS CLASSIFICATION

Consumer goods can be further classified by considering three characteristics: 1) the effort the consumer spends on the decision, 2) the attributes used in purchase, and 3) the frequency of purchase.

Convenience goods - Items the consumer uses frequently, conveniently and with a minimum of effort.

Shopping goods - Goods for which the consumer compares several alternatives on criteria such as price, quality, or style.

Specialty goods - Items which a consumer makes a special effort to search out and buy.

Classify the following type of consumer goods:

1. _____Breath Mints

2. _____Manicures

3. _____Jogging Shoes

4. _____Dry Cleaning

5. _____Pianos

6. _____Napkins

7. _____Burial plots

8. _____Life insurance

There may be differences in answers due to the relative importance of these items based on a person's own frame of reference.

* Challenge - Explain why and how one person may consider a product to be a shopping good while someone else may consider it a specialty good.

INDUSTRIAL GOODS CLASSIFICATION

"Industrial goods are classified not only on the attribute the consumer uses but also on how the item is to be used."

Production goods - Raw materials enter the manufacturing process of the final product completely, or as components.

Support goods - Items which are purchased to assist in the production of the final product.

I. Classify the following industrial goods:

1. _____Decals for model airplanes

2. _____Wood glue for fastening veneer

3. _____Tomatoes for ketchup

4. _____Glass for automobile windows

5. _____Wheat for bread

6. _____Coal for heating plant furnaces

7. _____An assembly line robot which performs spot welds

There are four types of support goods. These include:

Installations
Accessory equipment
Supplies
Services

II. Match the correct industrial support goods classification with the examples listed below:

1. _____Custodial work

2. _____Stock warehouses

3. _____Tool and die machine

4. _____Paper goods: towels, cups, toilet

   paper

5. _____Heating and cooling repair

6. _____Office chairs

WHAT IS A NEW PRODUCT?

The term "new" is difficult to define.

Newness compared with other products
Newness in legal terms
Newness from a company perspective
Newness from the consumer perspective

Match the correct perspective of newness to the examples below.

1. _____A revised item or totally new innovation. Example: automatic focus on 35 mm cameras or cellular car telephones.

2. _____The term "new" can be used by any product up to a twelve month period after it enters regular distribution.

3. _____If a product is functionally different from existing offerings. Example: the first Polaroid camera.

4. _____The newness is determined by the degree of learning required by the consumer. Example: learning to cook with a microwave.

NEWNESS FROM THE CONSUMER'S PERSPECTIVE

Newness from the consumer's perspective classifies new products according to the degree of learning required by the consumer.

Discontinuous innovation
Dynamically continuous innovation
Continuous new product

Match the correct term to the statements or examples listed below:

1. _____Although this product can be somewhat disruptive, totally new behaviour by the consumer is not required for its use.

2. _____No new behaviors must be learned.

3. _____Often a significant amount of time must be spent initially educating the consumer on how to use the product.

4. _____An example of this type of product newness is the advent of automatic transmissions.

5. _____An example of this type of product newness is the microwave oven.

6. _____An example of this type of product newness is the disposable straight razor.

NEW PRODUCTS AND WHY THEY FAIL

There are six fundamental reasons why products fail:

> Target market too small
> Insignificant point of difference
> Poor product quality
> No access to consumers
> Bad timing
> Poor execution of the marketing mix

Match the reason for failure to the statements or examples listed below:

1. _____Many pharmaceutical companies have facilities for research and development of new drugs for rare diseases. Unfortunately, since so few people have these diseases, it would be financially unsound to produce them. (Legislation is now being considered to help support "orphan drugs".)

2. _____A young musician goes on tour to promote his new album. The concerts are a huge success, but due to a problem in distribution, the records do not arrive in the music stores until six weeks after the concert.

3. _____Holly Farms new roasted chicken was edible for 18 days, but it took nine days to get from the production plant to the supermarket.

4. _____Duractin, an aspirin that gave eight hours of relief, lasted somewhat longer than other brands. However, people with headaches were more concerned with immediate relief than long-lasting relief.

5. _____When General Foods introduced Post Cereals with freeze-dried fruits, people found that by the time the fruit had absorbed enough milk, the flakes were soggy.

6. _____Some new products are actually superior to ones on the market but they may not have the budget to compete for available shelf space.

NEW PRODUCT STRATEGY DEVELOPMENT
PROACTIVE AND REACTIVE NEW PRODUCT STRATEGIES

There are two types of new product strategies:

    Proactive strategy
    Reactive strategy

Match the correct new product strategy to the statements below:

1. _____ Strategies which allocate resources to identify and seize opportunities which involve future-oriented research and development, consumer research, entrepreneurial development or acquisition.

2. _____ Strategies which require taking a defensive approach in response to a competitor's strategy.

3. _____ In response to IRI's videocart, Great Atlantic and Pacific Tea Company will start testing in-store electronic signs that will show ads and promotions.

4. _____ Spalding Sports Worldwide spent $1,000,000 developing a high-tech model tennis racket called the Pro Response Series.

DEVELOPING NEW PRODUCTS

There are seven steps in the new product process:

    New product development strategy
    Idea generation
    Screening and evaluation
    Business analysis
    Development
    Market-Testing
    Commercialization

Match the correct stage in the new product process with the examples below:

1. _____ In 1984 AT&T introduced its model 7300 Unix personal computer in order to establish a foothold in the business market for networked microcomputers, and to take advantage of the company's expertise in communication networks.

2. _____ In 1990 Peninsula Farms introduced a new line of ice cream in four stores in a regional market.

3. _____ If Peninsula Farms sales were favourable, then a full regional introduction would be sometime late in 1991.

4. _____ Many companies use their own checklist for quickly evaluating product ideas early in the development process.

5. _____ Hallmark Cards regularly solicits product ideas from members of its sales force through the use of a mail questionnaire.

6. _____ Medigas considers factors such as total market dollars, market growth rate, gross profitability, and cash flow in this stage of their new product process.

7. _____ At Mattel new product prototypes are "child-tested" in special testing playgrounds during this stage.

IDEA GENERATION

"Idea generation is a difficult step and must be conducted in light of the prior stage's objectives. New product ideas can be generated by customers, employees, basic research and development, and competitors."

List at least two examples of how these groups can generate new ideas:

Customers _____

_____

Employees _____

_____

Research & Development _____

_____

Competition _____

_____

SCREENING AND EVALUATION

*Challenge - Using Figure 9-7 in your text as a guideline, design a weighted point system. Choose a product new to the market and evaluate it according to your chart. It will be interesting to follow the success or failure of the product, and to see how accurately you evaluated its strengths and weaknesses.

BUSINESS ANALYSIS

Which of the following are performed at the business analysis stage of the new product process?

_____ A determination is made as to whether the new product will help or hurt sales of existing products.

_____ An assessment is made as to whether current distribution channels can be used or whether new channels will have to be developed.

_____ Costs for research and development are determined.

_____ Costs for production are determined.

_____ Forecasts are made for future sales.

_____ Forecasts are made for potential market share.

_____ A break-even analysis is performed.

_____ Estimates are made for return-on-investment to assess future profitability.

DEVELOPMENT

*Challenge - Many interesting articles have been written about the development stage of consumer products. Find an article of personal interest. (Save your example. It may come in handy someday.)

MARKET TESTING

Two elements in the testing stage of the new product process are:

Test marketing
Purchase laboratories

List the advantages and disadvantages for each technique.

Test Marketing

Advantages	Disadvantages
1. _____	1. _____
2. _____	2. _____
3. _____	3. _____
4. _____	4. _____

Purchase Laboratories

Advantages	Disadvantages
1. _____	1. _____
2. _____	2. _____

COMMERCIALIZATION

"Finally, the product idea is brought to the point of commercialization-launching the product in full scale production and sales."

1. To minimize financial risk if a market failure firms use _____.

2. A way of speeding up new product development is to use _____.

QUICK RECALL

I.   What are the three classifications of consumer goods?

        1. _____

        2. _____

        3. _____

II. What are the two classifications of industrial goods?

        1. _____

        2. _____

III.   What are the four types of support goods?

        1. _____

        2. _____

        3. _____

        4. _____

IV.   What are the four perspectives of newness?

1. _____

2. _____

3. _____

4. _____

V.   What are the three classifications of newness from the customer's perspective?

1. _____

2. _____

3. _____

VI.   Name six fundamental reasons why products fail.

1. _____

2. _____

3. _____

4. _____

5. _____

6. _____

II.   What are the seven steps in the new product process?

1. _____

2. _____

3. _____

4. _____

5. _____

6. _____

7. _____

VIII. Name four groups from which new product ideas are generated.

1. _____

2. _____

3. _____

4. _____

IX. Name two procedures for testing new products.

1. _____

2. _____

ANSWERS

TERMS AND DEFINITIONS

1. product
2. product mix
3. convenience goods
4. product line
5. consumer goods
6. shopping goods
7. new product process
8. new product strategy development
9. market testing
10. industrial goods
11. production goods

12. specialty goods
13. support goods
14. idea generation
15. business analysis
16. development
17. screening and evaluation
18. commercialization
19. unsought goods
20. proactive strategy
21. reactive strategy

PRODUCT LINE AND PRODUCT MIX

1. product mix
2. product line
3. product item
4. stock keeping unit

CLASSIFYING PRODUCTS

I. 1. nondurable
    2. services
    3. durable

    4. nondurable
    5. services
    6. durable

II. 1. industrial or consumer
    2. industrial
    3. industrial

    4. consumer or industrial
    5. industrial
    6. consumer

CONSUMER GOODS CLASSIFICATION

1. convenience good
2. specialty goods
3. shopping goods
4. convenience goods

5. specialty goods
6. convenience goods
7. unsought
8. unsought

INDUSTRIAL GOODS CLASSIFICATION

I. 1. production goods
    2. support goods
    3. production goods
    4. production goods

    5. production goods
    6. support goods
    7. support goods

II. 1. services
    2. installation
    3. installation

    4. support
    5. services
    6. accessories

WHAT IS A NEW PRODUCT?

1. company perspective
2. legal perspective
3. compared with other products
4. consumer perspective

NEWNESS FROM THE CONSUMER'S PERSPECTIVE

1. dynamically continuous innovation
2. continuous new product
3. discontinuous innovation
4. dynamically continuous innovation
5. discontinuous innovation
6. continuous new product

NEW PRODUCTS AND WHY THEY FAIL

1. target market too small
2. bad timing
3. bad timing
4. insignificant point of difference
5. poor product quality
6. no access to consumers

NEW PRODUCT STRATEGY DEVELOPMENT
PROACTIVE AND REACTIVE NEW PRODUCT STRATEGIES

1. proactive
2. reactive
3. reactive
4. proactive

DEVELOPING NEW PRODUCTS

1. new product development strategy
2. testing
3. commercialization
4. screening and evaluation
5. idea generation
6. business analysis
7. development

IDEA GENERATION

There are many possible correct answers. For further guidance refer to your text page(s): 241.

BUSINESS ANALYSIS

ALL of the choices are correct. All of these activities are performed at the business analysis stage of the new product process.

<u>MARKET TESTING</u>

Test Marketing

Possible Advantages

1. Poses less risk than introduction without testing.
2. Allows for product adjustment.
3. Can test other aspects of the mix.
4. Creates geographic distributing line for a national roll-out of a successful test product.

Possible Disadvantages

1. expensive
2. time consuming
3. reveals product to competitors
4. difficult to generalize results

Purchase Laboratories

Possible Advantages

1. less expensive
2. less time consuming

Possible Disadvantages

1. more artificial
2. does not provide a basis for market projection

<u>COMMERCIALIZATION</u>

1. regional rollouts
2. parallel development

<u>QUICK RECALL</u>

I.   1. convenience goods
     2. shopping goods
     3. specialty goods

II. 1. production goods
     2. support goods

III. 1. installation
     2. accessory equipment
     3. supplies
     4. services

IV. 1. compared with other products
     2. in legal terms
     3. from a company perspective
     4. from a consumer perspective

V.   1. discontinuous innovation
        2. dynamically continuous innovation
        3. continuous new product

VI.   1. too small a target market
        2. insignificant point of difference
        3. poor product quality
        4. no access to consumers
        5. bad timing
        6. poor execution of the marketing mix

VII.   1. new product strategy
        2. idea generation
        3. screening and evaluation
        4. business analysis
        5. development
        6. testing
        7. commercialization

VIII.   1. customers
        2. employees
        3. research and development
        4. competition

IX.   1. test marketing
        2. purchase laboratories

10

MANAGING THE PRODUCT

TERMS AND DEFINITIONS

Listed below are the definitions of important marketing terms. Choose the correct term for each definition from the list below, and write it in the space provided.

Branding
Brand mark
Generic brand
Licensing
Manufacturer branding
Marketing modification
Mixed branding
Multibranding
Multiproduct branding
Packaging
Private branding

Product class
Product form
Product life cycle
Product modification
Product repositioning
Trade name
Trademark
Trading down
Trading up
Warranty

1. _____ A concept which describes the stages a new product goes through in the marketplace: introduction, growth, maturity, and decline.

2. _____ Attempting to increase product usage by creating new use situations, finding new customers, or altering the marketing mix.

3. _____ Changing the place a product occupies in a consumer's mind relative to competitive products.

4. _____ An entire product category or industry.

5. _____ Strategies of altering a product characteristic, such as quality, performance, or appearance.

6. _____ Adding value to a product or line by including more features or higher quality materials.

7. _____ Legal identification of a company's exclusive rights to use a brand name, brand mark, or trade name.

8. _____ A manufacturer's branding strategy in which a distinct name is given to each product the company offers.

9. _____ A branding strategy in which a product is sold under the name of a wholesaler or retailer.

10. _____ A word or device (design, shape or colour) or combination of these used to distinguish a seller's goods or services.

11. _____ Reducing the number of features, quality, or price of a product.

12. _____ Variations of product within a product class.

13. _____ A branding strategy in which the brand name for a product is designated by the producer, using either a multiproduct or multibrand approach.

14. _____ A branding strategy in which a company uses one name for all products. Also referred to as blanket or family branding.

15. _____ Products given no identifying name other than a description of the contents.

16. _____ A statement indicating the liability of a manufacturer for product deficiencies.

17. _____ Activity in which an organization uses a name, phrase, design, or symbol to identify its products and distinguish them from those of a competitor.

18. _____ A commercial, legal name under which a company does business.

19. _____ The container in which a product is offered for sale and on which information is communicated.

20. _____ A branding strategy in which the company may follow both manufacturer and private (or reseller) branding approaches for products in their lines.

21. _____ A contractual agreement whereby a company allows someone else to use its brand name and usually requires the product be made to their specifications.

PRODUCT LIFE CYCLE

There are four distinct stages in the product life cycle. Each stage suggests its own distinct marketing strategy.

> Introduction
> Growth
> Maturity
> Decline

I.   Below are listed statements that describe different aspects of the four stages in the product life cycle. Decide which stage is being described in each statement below.

1. _____ To discourage competitive entry a company can price low, referred to as penetration.

2. _____ Heavy promotional expenditures are made to build primary demand.

3. _____ Promotional expenses at this stage are often directed towards contests or games to keep people using the product.

4. _____ Sales increase because of new users and a growing proportion of repeat purchasers.

5. _____ Sales and profits drop steadily.

6. _____ Often this stage is entered because of environmental or technological factors.

7. _____ Sales grow slowly and there is little profit, often a result of large investment costs.

8. _____ Emphasis of advertising shifts to selective demand.

9. _____ Improved versions or new features may be added to the original design.

10. _____ A high initial price may be used as part of a skimming strategy to help recover costs of development.

11. _____ During this stage companies are competing aggressively for shelf space.

12. _____ Profit declines since the cost of gaining each new buyer at this stage is greater than the incremental revenue.

13. _____ The company may follow the strategies of deletion, harvesting, or contracting in this stage.

II. Below are listed statements that describe different aspects of the four stages in the product life cycle. Decide which stage is being described in the statements below.

1. _____ During this stage the emphasis of advertising shifts to selective demand, product changes are made to help differentiate the brand from its competitors, and emphasis is put on gaining as much distribution as possible. VCR equipment is currently in this stage.

2. _____ During this stage a company wants to maintain its existing buyers because few new buyers are available to replace any who are lost. Colour television is in this stage.

3. _____ A marketing objective for a company at this stage is to promote consumer awareness. Sophisticated home exercise equipment is in this stage.

4. _____ At this stage a company may either drop the product from the line, retain the product but reduce support costs, or contract with a smaller company to manufacture the product. Video game units are currently in this stage.

III. "To handle a declining product, a company may follow one of three strategies:"

Deletion
Harvesting
Contracting

Match the strategy used in the decline stage of the product life cycle to the correct statement below:

1. _____ A strategy by which a company retains the product but reduces the support costs.

2. _____ A strategy by which a company drops a product from the line.

3. _____ A strategy by which a company makes an arrangement with another company to manufacture and/or market the product.

THE SHAPE OF THE LIFE CYCLE

"... There are a number of different life cycle curves, each type suggesting different marketing strategies."

There are four different life cycle curves:

High learning
Low learning
Fashion
Fad products

I.   Match the product life cycle with the statements below:

1. _____ Sales begin immediately, the benefits are readily understood.

2. _____ There is an extended introductory period during which significant education of the customer is required.

3. _____ Consumers have to be taught the benefits of the new product.

4. _____ These life cycles appear most frequently in women's and men's clothing styles and may vary in length from years to decades.

5. _____ This cycle has rapid sales upon introduction and usually equally rapid sales declines.

6. _____ The marketing strategy is to gain a strong distribution network at the beginning.

7. _____ Often this cycle rises, declines, then rises again.

8. _____ A perfect example of this was the Pet Rock.

II. Match the correct product life cycle to the graphs below:

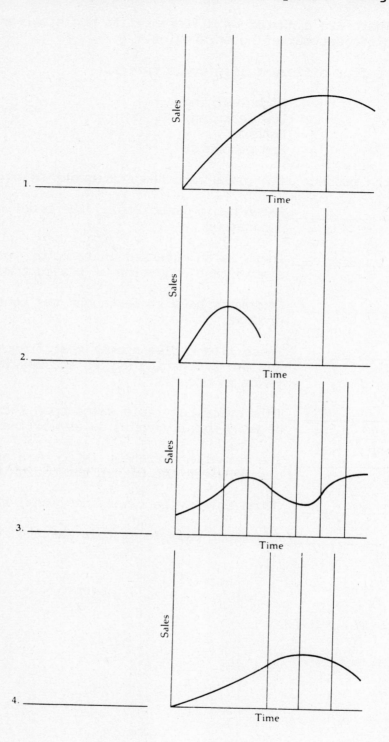

1. _____

2. _____

3. _____

4. _____

MODIFYING THE PRODUCT

"With marketing modification strategies, a company tries to increase a product's use among existing customers, to create new use situations, or to find new customers."

Decide whether the following statements are examples of:

Increasing use
Creating new use situations
Finding new users

1. _____ Tums antacid is now being advertised as an excellent calcium supplement.

2. _____ Arm and Hammer Baking Soda, marketed for years as a baking ingredient, is now being promoted as a deodorizer for cat litter, carpeting, and refrigerators.

3. _____ Revlon changed the name of its "Pretty Feet" lotion to "Pretty Hands and Feet."

4. _____ For years the makers of Dentyne chewing gum have advised people to chew Dentyne if they can't brush after every meal.

5. _____ Major North American car makers are offering buying incentives to newly graduated college students who traditionally have had little or no credit history.

6. _____ The manufacturer of a presweetened cereal is currently running an ad campaign targeted to adults.

*Challenge - Make a list of product slogans that demonstrate the three strategies listed in the previous exercise.

PRODUCT REPOSITIONING

"Product repositioning is changing the place a product occupies in a consumer's mind relative to competitive products. A firm can reposition a product by changing one or more of the four marketing mix elements."

There are several reasons for repositioning a product:

> Reacting to a competitor's position
> Reaching a new market
> Catching a rising trend
> Changing value offered

I.   Match the reason for repositioning with the following examples:

1. _____ Snickers candy bar was repositioned from a candy bar to a snack food which has twice as large a market.

2. _____ Mercedes traded down its line with the introduction of the Mercedes 190 sedan.

3. _____ Coke was repositioned as a slightly sweeter, less filling soft drink because Coca-Cola discovered that its 1984 market share in supermarkets was 2 percent behind Pepsi-Cola's.

4. _____ To reposition Marlboro cigarettes from female to male smokers, Philip Morris adopted a western image for the cigarette and ran ads featuring a cowboy.

II. "In repositioning the product line, a company can decide to change the value it offers buyers by trading up or trading down."

If you owned an automobile manufacturing company, list at least 3 ways you could reposition by trading up.

1. _____

2. _____

3. _____

If you owned a supermarket, list at least 3 ways you could reposition by trading down.

1. _____

2. _____

3. _____

BRANDING

"A brand is a name, symbol, term, design, or combination of these that distinguishes the seller's goods or services from a competitor's."

"A brand name is that part of the brand which can be spoken." For example: Coca-Cola.

"A brand mark is the symbol or design that cannot be vocalized." For example: the state of Texas outline on Texas Instruments Products.

I.   Make a list of twenty brand names and their corresponding brand marks. As a challenge - give a classmate only the brand names and have him or her describe the brand mark or give your classmate the brand marks only and have him or her identify the brand name.

II. List three advantages of branding.

1. _____

2. _____

3. _____

SELECTING A GOOD BRAND NAME

There are four criteria for selecting a good brand name.

The name should describe product benefits.
The name should be memorable, positive, and distinctive.
The name should fit the company or product image.
The name should have no legal restrictions.

I. List three examples of brand names which describe product benefits.

1. _____

2. _____

3. _____

II. List three examples of brand names which are memorable, positive, or distinctive.

1. _____

2. _____

3. _____

BRANDING STRATEGIES

"When making branding decisions, companies may use several possible branding strategies:

Manufacturer branding
Private branding
Mixed branding
Generic branding

I. Manufacturer branding

In manufacturer branding a manager can use either a multiproduct branding or multibranding strategy.

List the advantages and disadvantages of manufacturer's branding:

Multiproduct Branding

Advantages	Disadvantages
1. _____	1. _____
2. _____	2. _____
3. _____	3. _____

Multibranding

Advantages	Disadvantages
1. _____	1. _____
2. _____	2. _____
3. _____	3. _____

II.   Private branding

"A company uses private branding when it manufactures products but sells them under the brand name of a wholesaler or retailer."

What is the major advantage and disadvantage of private branding?

1. Advantage:

_____

_____

2. Disadvantage:

_____

_____

*Challenge - Make a list of manufacturers who use private branding.

III.   Mixed branding

"A compromise between the two previously described approaches is a mixed branding strategy."

What is the major rationale for using a mixed branding strategy?

_____

_____

_____

*Challenge - Compare a generic and brand name product in terms of price and quality.

PACKAGING

"The packaging component of a product refers to any container in which it is offered for sale and on which information is communicated."

There are three main benefits of packaging:

Communication benefits
Functional benefits
Perceptual benefits

I.   Make a list of all the <u>types</u> of information that can be communicated on a package. Use specific product examples. For example: product name.

1. _____   6. _____

2. _____   7. _____

3. _____   8. _____

4. _____   9. _____

5. _____   10. _____

II. Using products commonly found in a supermarket, make a list of at least ten different <u>types</u> of package. For example: cardboard box.

1. _____   6. _____

2. _____   7. _____

3. _____   8. _____

4. _____   9. _____

5. _____   10. _____

III.   Using items commonly found in a supermarket, select the single item's packages you feel connote the greatest <u>status</u>, <u>economy</u>, and <u>product quality</u>, and give your reasons for the selection.

1. Status   _____

2. Economy _____

3. Quality _____

*Challenge - Find an item whose package you find unsatisfactory. Write to the manufacturer giving not only your reasons for dissatisfaction but positive suggestions for improvement as well.

WARRANTIES

"A warranty is a statement indicating the liability of the manufacturer for product deficiencies."

Choose either a type of an automobile, a small appliance, or a service, and compare at least three different brands. List the characteristics of the warranties and choose which <u>warranty</u> you think is best. Give your reasons for your answer.

_____

_____

_____

_____

QUICK RECALL

I.   What are the four stages in the product life cycle?

     1. _____

     2. _____

     3. _____

     4. _____

II.   What are three different strategies for the decline stage of the product life cycle?

     1. _____

     2. _____

     3. _____

III.   What are four different types of product life cycles?

     1. _____

     2. _____

     3. _____

     4. _____

IV.   List the four types of branding strategies.

1. _____

2. _____

3. _____

4. _____

V.   What are three purposes of packaging?

1. _____

2. _____

3. _____

TERMS AND DEFINITIONS

1. product life cycle
2. marketing modification
3. product repositioning
4. product class
5. product modification
6. trading up
7. trademark
8. multibranding
9. private branding
10. brand name
11. trading down

12. product form
13. manufacturer branding
14. multiproduct branding
15. generic brands
16. warranty
17. branding
18. trade name
19. packaging
20. mixed branding
21. licensing

PRODUCT LIFE CYCLE

I.
1. introduction
2. introduction
3. maturity
4. growth
5. decline
6. decline
7. introduction

8. growth
9. growth
10. introduction
11. growth
12. maturity
13. decline

II.
1. growth
2. maturity
3. introduction
4. decline

III.
1. harvesting
2. deletion
3. contracting

THE SHAPE OF THE LIFE CYCLE

I.
1. low learning
2. high learning
3. high learning
4. fashion

5. fad products
6. low learning
7. fashion
8. fad products

II.
1. low learning
2. fad

3. fashion
4. high level

MODIFYING THE PRODUCT

1. Creating new use situations
2. Creating new use situations
3. Increasing use
4. Increasing use
5. Finding new customers
6. Finding new customers

PRODUCT REPOSITIONING

I.   1. catching a rising trend
     2. changing value offered
     3. reacting to a competitor's position
     4. reaching a new market

II.   There are many possible correct answers. For further guidance, refer
to your text page(s): 270-271

     1. Create a luxury model.
     2. Offer more upscale options for current models.
     3. Decrease factory defects and offer a 7 year warranty.

     1. Reduce store hours.
     2. Reduce number of brands carried.
     3. Operate on cash only basis.

BRANDING

I.   There are many possible correct answers. For further guidance, refer to
your text page(s): 271

II.   1. legal protection
      2. consumer loyalty
      3. identification

SELECTING A GOOD BRAND NAME

I, II There are many possible correct answers. For further guidance, refer
to your text page(s): 272-274

BRANDING STRATEGIES

I.   Manufacturer branding

Multiproduct Branding

   Advantages:

1. carry over of consumer good will
2. lower advertising costs
3. lower development costs

   Disadvantages:

1. carry over of poor performance
2. image dilution
3. more difficult to promote a specific product

Multibranding

Advantages:

1. lower risk of detrimental carry over effect
2. better able to promote specific products to specific segments
3. easier to reposition a specific product

Disadvantages:

1. promotional costs are higher
2. development costs are higher
3. no synergistic effects from identity with a family of brands

II. PRIVATE BRANDING

1. Promotional cost burden is shifted to the reseller.
2. Sales are heavily dependent upon the marketing capabilities of the reseller.

III. MIXED BRANDING

You can attract customers from several different segments.

PACKAGING

I.   There are many possible correct answers. For further guidance, refer to your text page(s): 277-279

Product name/brand name/trademark, price, UPC, weight, ingredients, quantity, dietary information, manufacturer's address, recipes, product illustration or picture, warranties, etc.

II.   There are many possible correct answers. For further guidance, refer to your text page(s): 277-279

Plastic bag, foil bag, paper bag, glass jar, cellophane wrapper, paper wrapper, foil wrapper, plastic carton, paper carton, plastic basket, paper tray, cardboard carton, aluminum can, etc.

III. There are many possible correct answers. For further guidance, refer to your text page(s): 277-279

1. status - Chanel's Black & Gold packaging
2. economy - Aim toothpaste pump
3. quality - Beck's silver foil beer bottle, Good Housekeeping Seal of Approval

WARRANTIES

Make sure your answer is based on printed information on packages and not "intuition" or personal bias.

QUICK RECALL

I.   1. introduction
     2. growth
     3. maturity
     4. decline

II. 1. Drop the product from the line (deletion).
     2. Retain the product but reduce support costs (harvesting).
     3. Contract with a smaller company to manufacture the product (contracting).

III. 1. high learning
     2. low learning
     3. fashion
     4. fad products

IV. 1. mixed branding
     2. private branding
     3. generic branding
     4. manufacturer branding

V.   1. communication benefits
     2. functional benefits
     3. perceptual benefits

11

PRICING: RELATING OBJECTIVES TO REVENUES AND COSTS

TERMS AND DEFINITIONS

Listed below are the definitions of important marketing terms. Choose the correct term for each definition from the list below, and write it in the space provided.

Average revenue
Break-even analysis
Break-even chart
Break-even point
Demand curve
Demand factors
Fixed cost
Marginal analysis
Marginal cost

Marginal revenue
Price
Price elasticity of demands
Pricing constraints
Pricing objectives
Profit equation
Total cost
Total revenue
Variable cost

1. _____ Factors that limit a firm's latitude in the price it may set.

2. _____ The average amount of money received for selling one unit of a product.

3. _____ The money or other considerations including other goods or services exchanged for the ownership or use of a good or service.

4. _____ The total money received from the sale of a product.

5. _____ Factors that determine consumers' willingness to pay for goods and services.

6. _____ Goals that specify the role of price in an organization's marketing and strategic plans.

7. _____ The change in total revenue obtained by selling one additional unit.

8. _____ Shows a maximum number of products consumers will buy at a given price.

9. _____ Principle of allocating resources that balances incremental returns of an action against incremental costs.

10. _____ An expense of the firm that is stable and does not change with the quantity of product that is produced and sold.

11._____The percentage change in quantity demanded relative to a percentage change in price.

12._____An expense of the firm that varies directly with the quantity of product produced and sold.

13._____The change in total cost that results from producing and marketing one additional unit.

14._____Profit = Total revenue minus Total cost.

15._____The total expense a firm incurs in producing and marketing a product; includes fixed costs and variable costs.

16._____A technique that analyzes the relationship between total revenue and total cost to determine profitability at various levels of output.

17._____Quantity at which total revenue and total cost are equal and beyond which profit occurs.

18._____A graphic presentation of a break-even analysis.

IDENTIFYING PRICING CONSTRAINTS

"Pricing constraints are factors that limit a firm's latitude in setting prices."

There are seven main factors which can be considered to be price constraints:

> Demand for the product class, product, or brand
> Newness of product in the product life cycle
> Single product vs. product line
> Cost of producing and marketing the product
> Cost of changing prices and time period to which they apply
> Type of competitive market
> Competitor's prices

Match the pricing constraint to the correct example:

1. _____ A cereal manufacturer prices all its oatmeal-based breakfast cereals within ten cents of each other.

2. _____ A recent survey in "Mademoiselle" magazine stated that 61 percent of the working women they surveyed are willing to spend more money for snack foods with fewer calories.

3. _____ Colour inserts for supermarket price promotions appear each Wednesday. The deadline for proof copy is the preceding Saturday.

4. _____ A product manager notices that 40 percent of his sales are coming from customers he classifies as laggards in the adoption process. He lowers his prices significantly to lure even more of them.

5. _____ Most public utilities must petition regulatory commissions in order to obtain a rate increase.

6. _____ It costs a consumer products company $700,000 to develop, test market, and introduce a new instant coffee.

7. _____ Texas Instruments was left with millions of dollars in lost revenue when it became involved in a price war and ended up selling units which originally sold for $1100 for $49.

IDENTIFYING PRICING OBJECTIVES

"Pricing objectives are goals that specify the role of price in an organization's marketing and strategic plans."

There are six main pricing objectives:

> Profit
> Sales
> Market share
> Survival
> Social responsibility
> Unit volume

These were also discussed briefly in Chapter 2.

Match the correct pricing objectives to the examples below:

1. _____ In the early 1980s Chrysler's president Lee Iacocca offered large cash rebates in order to maintain the firm's cash flow when unit sales were slumping.

2. _____ Medtronics, makers of the first heart pacemakers, placed its obligations to recipients above profits.

3. _____ In the rental car business, Hertz and Avis resorted to tie-in promotions with airlines in order to maintain their market position against National and Budget.

4. _____ Prior to the introduction of Datril, an identical and lower-priced acetaminophen product, Tylenol, was priced high in order to reap the highest possible revenue.

5. _____ A supermarket prices Yoplait yogourt at a point that produces the largest margin between cost and selling price.

6. _____ General Motors sought to reduce its car inventories through low interest car loans and rebates.

COMPETITIVE ENVIRONMENTS

"The type of market a product competes in affects pricing strategies."

Match the type of competitive environment with the following statements:

> Pure monopoly
> Oligopoly
> Monopolistic competition
> Pure competition

1. _____Many sellers who compete on non-price factors.

2. _____Few sellers who are sensitive to each other's prices.

3. _____One seller who sets the price for a unique product.

4. _____Many sellers who follow the market price for identical commodity products.

5. _____Sole seller sets price.

6. _____Market sets price.

7. _____Compete over a range of prices.

8. _____Price leader, or follower of competitors.

DEMAND CURVES

Below is a demand schedule showing the relationship between unit price and demand.

	UNIT PRICE (in dollars)	DEMAND (in units)
A.	250	200
B.	200	400
C.	150	600
D.	100	800
E.	50	1000

I. Plot a demand curve using the information listed above.

Price

|

Quantity

II. Determine total revenue at each point.

A = _____

B = _____

C = _____

D = _____

E = _____

III. Using the information in the first example, plot a total revenue curve.

Total
Revenue

|

Quantity

IV. Assuming a selling price of $50 per unit, fixed costs of $20,000, and a unit variable cost of $20, calculate the break-even point in dollars and units.

      1. BEP (Dollars) = _____

      2. BEP (Units) = _____

V. Identify the following parts of the profit maximizing graph below:

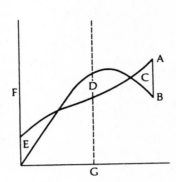

A. _____   E. _____

B. _____   F. _____

C. _____   G. _____

D. _____

PRICE ELASTICITY

"Price elasticity of demand (E) is defined as the percentage change in quantity demanded relative to a percentage change in price."

$$\text{Elasticity (E)} = \frac{Q_0 - Q_1}{Q_0} \quad \frac{P_0 - P_1}{P_0}$$

where, Q_0 = Initial quantity demanded

Q_1 = New quantity demanded

P_0 = Initial price

P_1 = New price

"Price elasticity of demand is not the same over all possible prices of the product."

Price elasticity may be expressed three ways.

1. If elasticity is greater than one, total revenue will be higher after a price decrease. The product demand is called "price elastic."

2. If elasticity is less than one, total revenue will be lower after a price decrease. The product demand is called "price inelastic."

3. If elasticity is equal to one, total revenue is the same as before, and the product demand is called "unitary elastic."

Using the information below, (A) calculate elasticity, and (B) determine if product demand is:

Elastic,
Inelastic, or
(has) Unitary Elasticity

Initial Quantity	10,000	1. Elasticity =	_____
New Quantity	12,000		
Initial Price	$2,000	Type =	_____
New Price	$1,000		

Initial Quantity	10,000	2. Elasticity =	_____
New Quantity	15,000		
Initial Price	$2,000	Type =	_____
New Price	$1,000		

Initial Quantity	10,000	3. Elasticity =	_____
New Quantity	30,000		
Initial Price	$2,000	Type =	_____
New Price	$1,000		

COST CONCEPTS

"Four cost concepts are important in pricing decisions . . ."

They are:

          Total cost
          Fixed cost
          Variable cost
          Marginal cost

Match the correct cost concept with the statement below:

1. _____ Total expenses incurred in producing and marketing the product.

2. _____ Change in total cost by producing and marketing one more unit.

3. _____ Expenses that are static regardless of the number of units marketed or produced.

4. _____ Expenses vary directly with quantity of product produced and sold.

THE DEMAND CURVE

"A Demand Curve shows the maximum number of products consumers will buy at a given price."

Use the following figure to answer the questions below:

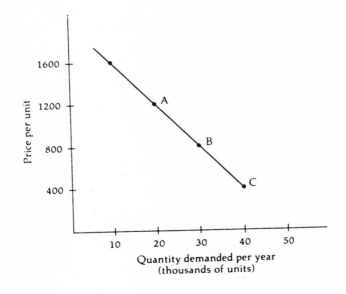

A. 1. _____At what price will the demand be 40,000?

   2. _____At what price will the demand be 10,000?

   3. _____What is the demand if the price is $800.00?

   4. _____What is the demand if the price is $1200.00?

*Challenge - Give at least three reasons which might account for a shift in the demand curve.

B. Using the graph from the previous example, find the average revenue for points A, B, and C.

1. A = _____

2. B = _____

3. C = _____

QUICK RECALL

I.   What are six major steps involved in setting prices?

   1. _____

   2. _____

   3. _____

   4. _____

   5. _____

   6. _____

II. What are seven factors to be considered as pricing constraints?

   1. _____

   2. _____

   3. _____

   4. _____

   5. _____

   6. _____

   7. _____

III. What are six major pricing objectives?

1. _____

2. _____

3. _____

4. _____

5. _____

6. _____

IV. What are the four types of competitive markets?

1. _____

2. _____

3. _____

4. _____

V. Make sure you can identify these letters in a marketing context.

TR	TC	MC	BEP	E
MR	FC	Q	UVC	SIC
AR	VC	P	PLC	

TERMS AND DEFINITIONS

1. pricing constraints
2. average revenue
3. price
4. total revenue
5. demand factors
6. pricing objective
7. marginal revenue
8. demand curve
9. marginal analysis

10. fixed cost
11. price elasticity of demand
12. variable cost
13. marginal cost
14. profit equation
15. total cost
16. break-even analysis
17. break-even point
18. break-even chart

IDENTIFYING PRICING CONSTRAINTS

1. single product vs. product line
2. demand for the product class, product or brand
3. cost of changing prices and time period they apply
4. newness of product in product life cycle
5. type of competitive market
6. cost of producing and marketing the product
7. competitors pricing

IDENTIFYING PRICING OBJECTIVES

1. survival
2. social responsibility
3. market share

4. sales
5. profit
6. unit volume

COMPETITIVE ENVIRONMENTS

1. monopolistic competition
2. oligopoly
3. pure monopoly
4. pure competition

5. pure monopoly
6. pure competition
7. monopolistic competition
8. oligopoly

DEMAND CURVES

I.

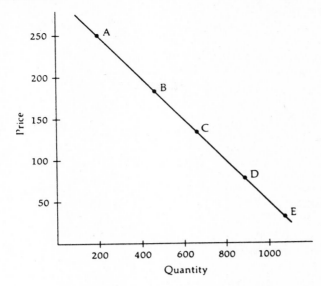

II.   A. $50,000   C. $90,000   E. $50,000
           B. $80,000   D. $80,000

III.

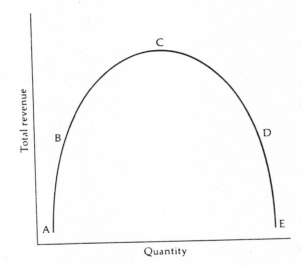

IV.   1. BEP (dollars) = $20,000/(1 - .4) = $33,333.33
           2. BEP (units) = $20,000/(50 - 20) = 666.67

V.   A. total cost curve   E. loss
          B. total revenue curve   F. dollar revenue or cost
          C. loss   G. quantity
          D. profit

PRICE ELASTICITY

1. 0.4, inelastic
2. 1.0, unitary elasticity
3. 4.0, elastic

COST CONCEPTS

1. total cost
2. marginal cost

3. fixed cost
4. variable cost

THE DEMAND CURVE

A. 1. $400
2. $1,600
3. 30,000 units
4. 20,000 units

B. 1. $1,200
2. $800
3. $400

QUICK RECALL

I.
1. identify price constraints and objectives
2. estimate demand and revenue
3. determine cost, volume, and profit relationships
4. select an appropriate price level
5. set list or quoted price
6. make special adjustments to list or quoted price

II.
1. demand for the product class, product, or brand
2. newness of product in product life cycle
3. single product vs. product line
4. cost of producing and marketing the product
5. cost of changing prices and time period they apply.
6. type of competitive market.
7. competitive pricing

III.
1. profit
2. sales
3. market share

4. survival
5. social responsibility
6. unit volume

IV.
1. pure monopoly
2. oligopoly

3. monopolistic
4. pure competition

12

PRICING: ARRIVING AT A FINAL PRICE

TERMS AND DEFINITIONS

Listed below are the definitions of important marketing terms. Choose the correct term for each definition from the list below, and write it in the space provided.

Above-, at-, or below-market pricing
Basing-point pricing
Bundle-pricing
Cost-plus fixed-fee pricing
Cost-plus percentage-of-cost pricing
Customary pricing
Demand-backward pricing
Experience curve pricing
Flexible-price policy
FOB origin policy
Loss-leader pricing
Odd-even pricing
One-price policy
Penetration pricing

Predatory pricing
Prestige pricing
Price discrimination
Price lining
Price-fixing
Promotional allowances
Quantity discounts
Sealed-bid pricing
Skimming pricing
Standard markup pricing
Target profit pricing
Target return-on-investment pricing
Target return-on-sales pricing
Uniform delivered pricing

1. _____ Setting the highest initial price that customers really desiring the product are willing to pay.

2. _____ The deliberate pricing of a product below its customary price to attract attention to it.

3. _____ Setting the same price for similar customers who buy the same product and quantities under the same conditions.

4. _____ Setting a high price so status-conscious consumers will be attracted to the product.

5. _____ A method of pricing where price often falls following the reduction of costs associated with the firm's experience in producing or selling a product.

6. _____ The reduction in unit costs for a larger order.

7. _____ Setting the price of a line's products at a number of different specific pricing points.

8. _____ A method of pricing where the title of goods passes to the buyer at the point of loading.

9. _____ A pricing strategy of setting a low initial price to discourage new competitors as well as to build market share.

10. _____ Setting prices a few dollars or cents under an even number.

11. _____ Setting prices to achieve a profit that is a specified percentage of the sales volume.

_____ Setting a price based on an annual specific dollar target volume of profit.

13. _____ Offering the same product and quantities to similar customers but at different prices.

14. _____ Results in the deliberate adjustment of quality and price of component parts to achieve a target price.

15. _____ Setting prices by adding a fixed percentage to the cost of all items in a specific product class.

16. _____ A method of pricing based on a product's tradition, standard channel of distribution, or other competitive factors.

17. _____ A pricing method where a supplier is reimbursed for all costs, regardless of what they may be, plus a fixed percentage of the production or construction cost.

18. _____ A pricing method based on what the "market price" is.

19. _____ A method of pricing where by prospective firms submit price bids to the buying agency at a specific time and place with the contract awarded to the qualified bidder with the lowest price.

20. _____ The cash payment or extra amount of "free goods" awarded sellers in the channel of distribution for undertaking certain advertising or selling activities to promote a product.

21. _____ A uniform delivered pricing method where the price the seller quotes includes all transportation costs.

22. _____ A method of setting prices to achieve a specific return on investment.

23. _____ Setting the price of a product or service by adding a fixed percentage to the production or construction cost.

24. _____ The marketing of two or more products in a single "package" price.

25. _____ A conspiracy among firms to set prices for a product.

26. _____ The practice of charging different prices to different buyers for goods of like grade and quality.

27. _____ The practice of charging a very low price for a product with the intent of driving competitors out of business.

28. _____ Selecting one or more geographical locations from which the list price for products plus freight expenses are charged to the buyers.

DEMAND-BASED METHODS

"Demand-based methods of finding a price level weigh factors underlying expected customer tastes more heavily than factors such as cost, profit, and competition."

There are six demand-based techniques for selecting an approximate price level:

> Skimming
> Penetration
> Prestige
> Price lining
> Odd-even
> Demand-backward
> Bundle pricing

Match the correct demand-based method with the examples below:

1. _____ Texas Instruments intentionally priced its hand-held calculators and digital watches extremely low in order to make them immediately appealing to the mass market.

2. _____ A large discount shoe company carries numerous brands of shoes. In order to make it easier for retailers and consumers, shoe prices are limited to only four pricing points.

3. _____ A famous chocolatier charged an extremely high price for a chocolate chip cookie that had excellent taste and texture but only ten calories. The next best cookie by a competitor had 35 calories.

4. _____ Two shirts of identical quality and construction have a price discrepancy of $10.00 because one of them has a small applique near the pocket.

5. _____ABC Food Systems decided that consumers would willingly pay $99.95 for a food dehydrator. Based on this price they determined margins that would have to be paid to wholesalers and retailers.

6. _____Several major hotel chains have offered a weekend getaway for only $49.95.

7. _____Some cake mixes are sold with the baking pan and icing included.

COST-BASED METHODS

"In cost-based methods, the price setter's emphasis is on the supply or cost side of the pricing problem, not on the demand side."

There are four cost-based methods:

> Standard mark-up
> Cost plus percentage-of-cost
> Cost plus fixed-fee
> Experience curve

Match the correct cost-based method with the examples below:

1. _____A convenience store carries hundreds of items. Rather than computing price differences for each item, a fixed percentage of 15 percent is added to the cost of staple items and 40 percent is added to the cost of discretionary items.

2. _____An eccentric millionaire custom orders a luxury sedan equipped with a foam and water waterbed and genuine chinchilla fur seat covers. The car manufacturer charges him for all costs (including procuring the chinchilla fur), regardless of what those costs may be, plus an additional fee of $8,000.

3. _____Digital watches once selling for $2,000.00 now sell for as little as $10.00. As demand has increased and production has doubled again and again, production, advertising, and selling costs declined.

4. _____A construction firm is anxious to bid on a tract of homes that will cost approximately $150,000 to build. After including the construction firm's fee of 15 percent, the final homes will sell for $172,500 each.

PROFIT-BASED METHODS

"A price setter may choose to balance both revenues and costs to set price using profit-based methods."

There are three profit-based methods:

> Target profit
> Target return-on-sales
> Target return-on-investment

Match the correct profit-based method with the examples below:

1. _____ The owner of a store specializing in gourmet cookware wants to be sure he realizes a profit of 25 percent on all goods shipped from France. He applies the formula 25 percent = (TR-TC)/TR to determine his prices.

2. _____ A craftsman makes wooden hobby horses in his spare time. In order to quit his full-time job he has to be able to make $12,000 profit per year. By inserting the amount $12,000 into the formula P=TR-TC he concludes he must sell 200 units at $140 apiece.

3. _____ Because of an oil shortage a plastic products manufacturer will have to pay twice as much this year as she did last year for petroleum-based production materials. In order to stay in business her prices and sales must reflect this change. She uses a computer spreadsheet to determine the best method of ensuring an 18 percent ROI before taxes.

COMPETITION-BASED METHODS

"Rather than emphasize demand, cost, or profit factors, a price setter can stress what competitors or 'the markets' are doing."

There are four competition-based methods:

Customary pricing
Above-, at-, or below-market pricing
Loss leader pricing
Sealed bid pricing

Match the correct competition-based method with the examples below.

1. _____Rolex takes pride in emphasizing that it makes one of the most expensive watches you can buy.

2. _____An independent grocer sold canned soft drinks at 12 for a dollar during the Labour Day Weekend in hopes that customers would buy other higher-priced barbecue and picnic items as well.

3. _____Most local school districts place an ad in the newspaper listing job specifications and qualifications for major contracts to ensure they receive the best offer at the best price. These offers are made by a certain date and kept confidential until the ultimate buying decision is made.

4. _____A candy manufacturer had to decide whether to make larger gumballs and charge a nickel, make smaller gumballs and keep the price at a penny, or switch to a different confection altogether that could be adapted to dispensers already found in grocery stores, etc.

SELECTING AN APPROPRIATE PRICE LEVEL

"There are four common methods used to find approximate price levels."

Decide whether the following methods are:

Demand-based
Cost-based
Profit-based
Competition-based

1. _____standard mark-up

2. _____skimming

3. _____target-profit

4. _____experience curve

5. _____target return-on-sales

6. _____penetration

7. _____prestige

8. _____customary

9. _____cost plus fixed percentage-of-cost

10. _____loss leader

11. _____odd-even

12. _____above-, at-, or below-market

13. _____cost plus fixed-fee

14. _____sealed bid

15. _____price lining

16. _____target return-on-investment

17. _____demand-backward

*Challenge - Identify several reasons why it is "good business" to consider using more than one pricing method.

SPECIAL ADJUSTMENTS TO LIST OR QUOTED PRICE

"There are three types of special adjustments that can be made to list or quoted prices."

Discounts
Allowances
Geographic adjustments

I.   Match the type of special adjustment to the examples listed below:

1. _____ A bathing suit manufacturer offered a 20 percent reduction in price to retailers placing their orders by January 16th.

2. _____ A pizza parlour issued special lunch cards. Every time a patron had lunch at the parlour, his card was stamped. Whenever a card had twelve stamps the patron received a free pizza for lunch.

3. _____ A manufacturer of garden tools using wholesalers and retailers quoted his price as list price less /30/15/.

4. _____ A supermarket manager agrees to promote a new line of sugar-free gum by sponsoring a "bubble-blowing contest." In appreciation, the manufacturer sends one free case of gum for each three purchases.

5. _____ A gas station chain offers its customers a lower price on gas if they pay cash instead of using credit cards.

6. _____ A supermarket offered a special price on new brooms to customers who brought their old brooms to the store. The old brooms were displayed by the door next to a barrel of new brooms.

7. _____ A telephone company offered a special rate of ten dollars an hour for phone calls anywhere in Canada.

8. _____ A company that sells materials for "build-it-yourself" homes charges a different fee depending upon how far you live from their warehouses.

9. _____ Many cruise lines pay the customers' air fare from the nearest major airport to the point of cruise departure.

II. Using the same examples as in exercise I, determine the correct _type_ of discount, allowance, or geographic adjustment using the terms listed below.

          Quantity discount   Trade-in allowance
          Seasonal discount   Promotional allowance
          Trade discount   F.O.B. origin pricing
          Cash discount   Uniform Delivered pricing

1. _____

2. _____

3. _____

4. _____

5. _____

6. _____

7. _____

8. _____

9. _____

LEGAL AND REGULATORY ASPECTS OF PRICING

There are four important practices that can be considered illegal.

          Price fixing
          Price discrimination
          Deceptive pricing
          Predatory pricing

Match the illegal pricing practice with the example below:

1. _____ Two firms who control their market get together and agree to price their products the same.

2. _____ A firm advertises a T.V. for $99 but when you arrive there is none available. You are then offered a $299. T.V.

3. _____ A manufacturer doesn't like you personally or how you run your business so you are charged 20% more for goods then your competitor two doors down.

4. _____ A well established competitor doesn't like the fact that you have opened a new business to compete with them. They decide to drastically cut their prices, taking a loss, to secure and retain business.

I.   Name four methods of selecting an approximate price level.

       1._____

       2._____

       3._____

       4._____

II.   List seven methods of demand-based pricing.

       1._____

       2._____

       3._____

       4._____

       5._____

       6._____

       7._____

III.   List four methods of cost-based pricing.

       1._____

       2._____

       3._____

       4._____

IV.   List three methods of profit-based pricing.

       1._____

       2._____

       3._____

V.   List four methods of competition-based pricing.

1._____

2._____

3._____

4._____

VI.   List four important factors to consider when setting the list or quoted price.

1._____

2._____

3._____

4._____

VII.   List three special adjustments that can be made to the list or quoted price.

1._____

2._____

3._____

VIII.   List four types of discounts.

1._____

2._____

3._____

4._____

IX.   List two types of allowances.

1._____

2._____

X.   List two types of geographic adjustments.

1._____

2._____

XI.   List four pricing practices that are regulated to maintain legality.

1._____

2._____

3._____

4._____

ANSWERS

TERMS AND DEFINITIONS

1. skimming pricing
2. loss-leader pricing
3. one-price policy
4. prestige pricing
5. experience curve
6. quantity discount
7. price lining
8. F.O.B. origin pricing
9. penetration pricing
10. odd-even pricing
11. target return on sales pricing
12. target profit
13. flexible pricing policy
14. demand-backward pricing
15. standard mark-up
16. customary pricing
17. cost plus fixed-fee pricing
18. above-at-below market pricing
19. sealed-bid pricing
20. promotional allowance
21. uniform delivered pricing
22. target return on investment
23. cost plus percentage-of-cost
24. bundle pricing
25. price fixing
26. price discrimination
27. predatory pricing
28. basing-point pricing

DEMAND-BASED METHODS

1. penetration
2. price lining
3. skimming
4. prestige
5. demand backward
6. odd-even
7. bundle pricing

COST-BASED METHODS

1. standard mark-up
2. cost plus fixed fee
3. experience curve
4. cost plus percentage of cost

PROFIT-BASED METHODS

1. target return on sales
2. target profit
3. target return on investments

COMPETITION-BASED METHODS

1. above-at-below market pricing
2. loss-leader
3. sealed bids
4. customary pricing

SELECTING AN APPROPRIATE PRICE LEVEL

1. cost based
2. demand based
3. profit based
4. cost based
5. profit based
6. demand based
7. demand based
8. competition based

9. cost based
10. competition based
11. demand based
12. competition based
13. cost based
14. competition based
15. demand based
16. profit based
17. demand based

SPECIAL ADJUSTMENTS TO LIST OR QUOTED PRICE

I.
1. discount
2. discount
3. discount
4. allowance
5. discount

6. allowance
7. geographic adjustment
8. geographic adjustment
9. geographic adjustment

II.
1. seasonal discount
2. quantity discount
3. trade (functional) discount
4. promotional allowance
5. cash discount

6. trade-in allowance
7. uniform delivered pricing
8. F.O.B. origin
9. delivered pricing

LEGAL AND REGULATORY ASPECTS OF PRICING

1. Price fixing
2. Deceptive pricing
3. Price discrimination
4. Predatory pricing

QUICK RECALL

I.
1. demand
2. cost

3. profit
4. competition

II.
1. skimming pricing
2. penetration pricing
3. prestige pricing
4. price lining pricing

5. odd-even pricing
6. demand backward pricing
7. bundle pricing

III.
1. standard mark-up
2. cost plus percentage of cost

3. cost plus fixed fee
4. experience curve

IV.
1. target profit
2. target return on sales
3. target return on investment

V.
1. customary pricing
2. above-at-below market pricing

3. loss leader pricing
4. sealed bids

VI.   1. one price vs. flexible price
        2. price to cover cost plus profit
        3. balance increased cost and revenue
        4. effect of the three C's

VII.   1. discounts
        2. allowances
        3. geographic adjustments

VIII.   1. quantity
        2. seasonal
        3. trade
        4. cash

IX.   1. trade-in
        2. promotional

X.   1. F.O.B.
        2. uniform delivered pricing

XI.   1. price discrimination
        2. price fixing
        3. predatory pricing
        4. deceptive pricing

13

MARKETING CHANNELS AND WHOLESALING

TERMS AND DEFINITIONS

Listed below are the definitions of important marketing terms. Choose the correct term for each definition from the list below, and write it in the space provided.

Brokers
Cash and carry wholesalers
Channel captain
Direct channel
Direct marketing
Drop shippers
Dual distribution
Exclusive distribution
Franchising
General merchandise wholesalers
Indirect channel

Industrial distributor
Intensive distribution
Manufacturer's agents
Marketing channel
Rack jobbers
Selective distribution
Selling agents
Specialty merchandise
 wholesalers
Truck jobbers
Vertical marketing systems

1. _____ Performs a variety of marketing channel functions, including selling, stocking, financing, and delivering a full product assortment.

2. _____ Producers and ultimate consumers interact directly with each.

3. _____ Individuals and firms involved in the process of making a product or service available for use or consumption by consumers or industrial users.

4. _____ A type of marketing channel that has intermediaries situated between producer and consumers.

5. _____ Small merchant wholesalers that usually handle limited assortments of fast-moving or perishable items that are sold directly from trucks for cash.

6. _____ Represent a single producer and are responsible for the entire marketing function of that producer.

7. _____ Full-service merchant wholesalers that carry a broad assortment of merchandise and perform all channel functions.

8. _____ The contractual arrangement between a parent company and an individual or firm that allows that person or firm to operate a certain type of business under an established name, and according to specific rules.

9. _____ Full-service merchant wholesalers that offer a relatively narrow range of products but carry extensive assortments within the product lines carried.

10. _____ A marketing channel member who coordinates, directs, and supports other channel members.

11. _____ An arrangement in which a firm reaches buyers by employing two or more different types of channels for the same basic product.

12. _____ A distribution strategy whereby a producer sells its products or services in only one retail outlet in a specific geographic area.

13. _____ An individual or firm that works for several producers and sells noncompetitive, complementary merchandise in an exclusive territory.

14. _____ A distribution strategy whereby a producer selects a few retail outlets in a specific area to carry its products.

15. _____ Independent firms or individuals whose principal function is to bring buyers and sellers together to make sales.

16. _____ A distribution strategy whereby a producer sells products or services in as many outlets as possible.

17. _____ A merchant wholesaler that owns the merchandise it sells, but does not physically handle, stock, or deliver it.

18. _____ Wholesalers that take titles to the merchandise, but sell only to buyers who call on them, pay cash for merchandise, and furnish their own transportation for merchandise.

19. _____ Professionally managed and centrally coordinated marketing channels designed to achieve channel function economies and maximum marketing impact.

20. _____ Wholesalers that furnish the display racks or shelves in retail stores; they generally sell on consignment.

21. _____ A method by which consumers buy products by interacting with various advertising media without a face-to-face meeting with a salesperson.

DEFINING MARKETING CHANNELS OF DISTRIBUTION

Marketing channels are individuals and firms involved in the process of making a product or service available for use or consumption by consumers or industrial users.

> Middleman
> Agent or Broker
> Wholesaler
> Retailer
> Distributor
> Dealer

1. _____ A middleman who sells to consumers.

2. _____ A term that can mean the same as distributor, retailer, wholesaler, and so forth; virtually synonymous with middleman.

3. _____ Any intermediary between manufacturer and end user markets.

4. _____ A middleman who sells to other middlemen, usually to retailers; usually applies to consumer markets.

5. _____ A middleman who performs a variety of distribution functions, including selling, maintaining inventories, extending credit, and so on; a more common term in industrial markets but may also be used to refer to wholesalers.

6. _____ Any middleman with legal authority to act on behalf of the manufacturer.

RATIONALE FOR INTERMEDIARIES

". . . intermediaries make selling products and services more efficient because they minimize the number of sales contacts." This reduces producer costs and hence benefits the consumer.

"Intermediaries make possible the flow of products and services from producers to buyers by performing three basic functions." They are:

    Transactional functions
    Logistical functions
    Facilitating functions

Decide whether the following functions are transactional, logistical, or facilitating functions:

1. _____marketing information and research

2. _____sorting

3. _____risk taking

4. _____buying

5. _____storing

6. _____financing

7. _____grading

8. _____transporting

9. _____assorting

10. _____selling

UTILITIES CREATED BY INTERMEDIARIES

"Having the products and services you want, when you want them, where you want them, and in the form you want them, is the ideal result of marketing channels."

There are four utilities created by intermediaries:

    Time
    Place
    Form
    Possession

Match the type of utility with the examples or statements listed below.

1. _____The Bay Department Store in Halifax provides tailoring and alteration services.

2. _____Many florists have branch outlets in or close to local hospitals.

3. _____Federal Express provides next morning delivery.

4. _____Joe situates his stores along highways to provide clean facilities and good food to travelers on long trips.

5. _____JL's IGA will smoke all types of meats for their customers.

6. _____A local drugstore stays open 24 hours a day to make sure it can accommodate customers in case of emergencies in the middle of the night.

7. _____A furniture manufacturer offers terms of "90 days same as cash."

8. _____A car dealership offers instant credit to college graduates who can provide a letter of job acceptance.

MERCHANT WHOLESALERS

"There are two main types of merchant wholesalers: full-service wholesalers and limited-service wholesalers."

I.   Indicate whether the following wholesalers are full-service wholesalers or limited-service wholesalers.

1. _____drop shipper

2. _____rack jobber

3. _____general merchandise

4. _____cash and carry

5. _____truck jobbers

6. _____specialty merchandise

II. Match the specific type of wholesaler to the examples below:

Drop shipper
Rack jobber
General merchandise
Cash and carry
Truck jobber
Specialty merchandise

1. _____ Mr. Green owns a hardware company. He carries a broad assortment of merchandise ranging from hand tools to kitchen supplies. However, he does not carry a great assortment within any single product line.

2. _____ Mrs. Sharp owns a company that specializes in cutlery. Although she sells only knives and scissors, she carries virtually every type of knife or scissor one could ask for.

3. _____ A company in the lumber business is located in an office in a high rise building in Toronto. Although they neither stock, handle, nor deliver the lumber themselves, they solicit orders from retailers and wholesalers and have the merchandise shipped directly from producers to buyers.

4. _____ A seafood wholesaler purchases fresh fish from local fishermen. He in turn sells the fish to restaurants who call on him, pay cash for their purchases, and pick the fish/seafood up themselves.

5. _____ John Smith distributes dairy items to small grocers in a metropolitan area. The drivers of his six trucks make deliveries once a day and all transactions are strictly cash.

6. _____ A company distributes snack foods to business office cafeterias. The snacks are displayed in a free-standing cardboard rack. The offices are billed only for the snack foods used.

AGENTS AND BROKERS

"Unlike merchant wholesalers, agents and brokers do not take title to merchandise, and typically provide fewer channel functions. They make their profit from commissions or fees paid for their services."

Manufacturer's agents
Selling agents
Brokers

Match the correct term listed above with the statements listed below:

1. _____ They design promotional plans, set prices, determine distribution policies, and make recommendations on product strategy.

2. _____ They usually do not have a continuous relationship with the buyer or seller. Rather, they negotiate a contract or deal between two parties, then move on to another task.

3. _____ They work for several producers and sell noncompetitive, complementary merchandise in an exclusive territory.

4. _____ They are principally used in transactional channel functions, primarily selling.

5. _____ They represent a single producer and are responsible for the entire marketing function of that producer.

6. _____ They are independent firms or individuals whose principal function is to bring buyers and sellers together to make a sales transaction.

MANUFACTURER'S BRANCHES AND OFFICES

"Unlike merchant wholesalers, agents, and brokers, manufacturer's branches and offices are wholly-owned extensions of the producer that perform wholesaling activities."

I.   List three characteristics of a manufacturer's branch office.

1. _____

2. _____

3. _____

II. List three characteristics of a manufacturer's sales office.

1. _____

2. _____

3. _____

VERTICAL MARKETING SYSTEMS (VMS)

"A Corporate vertical marketing system is a combination of successive stages of production and distribution under a single ownership."

I.   A corporate vertical marketing system may use either forward or backward integration. Match the correct term with the examples or statements listed below.

Forward integration
Backward integration

1. _____Sears owns a substantial share of Whirlpool, on whom it depends for its Kenmore appliances.

2. _____Sherwin Williams distributes its paint through a system of company-owned retail outlets.

3. _____Safeway operates its own Bakeries to supply its stores.

4. _____Goodyear manufactures tires and also owns retail tire stores.

II.   What is the major difference between corporate systems and administered systems?

_____

_____

_____

"Under a contractual vertical marketing system, independent production and distribution firms integrate their efforts on a contractual basis to obtain greater functional economies and marketing impact than they could achieve alone."

Three variations of contractual marketing systems exist:

> Wholesaler-sponsored voluntary chains
> Retailer-sponsored cooperatives
> Franchising

III. Match the correct form of contractual marketing system with the statements below:

1. _____ Ford Motor Corporation licenses dealers to sell its cars subject to various sales and service conditions.

2. _____ The Associated Grocers is a group of small independent retailers which formed an organization that operates a wholesale facility cooperatively. They concentrate their buying power through the wholesaler and plan collaborative promotional and pricing activities.

3. _____ Wholesalers who contract with smaller, independent retailers to standardize and coordinate buying practices, merchandising programs, and inventory management. I.G.A. is an example.

4. _____ H & R Block licenses individuals or firms to provide tax preparation services to the public.

FACTORS AFFECTING CHANNEL CHOICE AND MANAGEMENT

"The final choice of a marketing channel by a producer depends upon a number of factors that often interact with each other." They include:

> Environmental factors
> Consumer factors
> Product factors
> Company factors

Match the correct marketing channel factors with the statements or examples listed below:

1. _____ Ricoh Company, Ltd., studied information concerning the "serious" as opposed to "recreational" camera user, and decided to change its marketing channel from a wholesaler to a manufacturer's agent. Sales volume tripled within 18 months.

13-9

2. _____ When Ingersoll-Rand's pneumatic tools were first introduced, considerable buyer education and service were necessary to market these products, and a direct channel was used. As the products matured and buyers became more familiar with them, the company elected to use industrial distributors.

3. _____ IBM distributes its correctable typewriter ribbons directly through its own sales force. Liquid Paper Corporation, partially because of more limited resources and a narrower product line, uses indirect channels.

4. _____ Because of changes in economic factors, family structure, etc., companies such as Mary Kay and Tupperware are examining their current direct marketing channel strategies.

CHANNEL DESIGN CONSIDERATIONS

There are three types of distribution density:

    Intensive distribution
    Selective distribution
    Exclusive distribution

Match the type of distribution density to the statements below.

1. _____ Only one retail outlet in a specified geographic area carries the firm's products.

2. _____ A firm tries to place its products or services in as many outlets as possible.

3. _____ A firm selects only a few retail outlets in a specific area to carry its products.

4. _____ BMW uses this approach in order to maintain product image and also to have more control over the selling effort of its dealers.

5. _____ Hallmark Cards is able to maintain good dealer relationships because it limits the number and maintains the quality of outlets it sells through.

6. _____ Convenience goods are typically distributed in this manner.

CHANNEL DESIGN CONSIDERATIONS

There are three main considerations affecting Channel Design:

Target market coverage
Satisfying buyer requirements
Profitability

Match the consideration affecting channel design with the statements or examples listed below.

1. _____ "Ford, General Motors, and Honda have recently established new dealers for their new European line of expensive cars to reach the 'Yuppie' market . . ."

2. _____ Companies must decide the best way to satisfy needs for information, convenience, variety, and attendant services.

3. _____ A new company has to decide which Marketing Channel to use. They have to take into consideration costs of distribution, advertising, and selling expenses, relative to revenues generated.

CHANNEL RELATIONSHIPS

"Two types of conflict occur in marketing channels: vertical conflict and horizontal conflict."

Decide whether the following statements are examples of vertical conflict or horizontal conflict:

1. _____ H.J. Heinz Company is embroiled in a conflict with its supermarkets in Great Britain because the supermarkets are promoting and displaying private brands at the expense of Heinz brands.

2. _____ The owner of a downtown McDonald's complained vehemently to the franchiser when he learned that plans for the new enclosed mall included another McDonald's Restaurant.

3. _____ Friction emerged between Chrysler and its dealers when the company expected dealers to shoulder the burden of its $500 rebate program.

4. _____ K-Mart store managers complained to Kenner that another store was getting faster delivery during the holiday rush period.

*Challenge - Explain what a channel captain is, and how the captain emerges as such. Provide an example.

CHANNEL STRATEGIES AND PRACTICES AFFECTED BY LEGAL RESTRICTIONS

Conflict in marketing channels is typically resolved through negotiation or the exercise of power by channel members. Sometimes conflict produces legal action.

Vertical integration
Tying arrangements
Resale restrictions
Refusal to deal
Exclusive dealing
Dual distribution

Match the correct term to the appropriate channel strategy or practice.

1. _____ When a manufacturer distributes through its own vertically integrated channel in competition with independent wholesalers and retailers that also sell its products.

2. _____ This practice is sometimes subject to legal action if it has the potential to lessen competition or foster monopoly.

3. _____ When a supplier requires channel members to sell only its products or restricts distributors from selling directly competitive products.

4. _____ This occurs when a supplier requires a distributor to purchase some products on the condition it buy others from the supplier.

5. _____ Refers to a supplier's attempt to stipulate to whom distributors may resell the supplier's products and in what specific geographical areas or territories they may be sold.

6. _____ Choosing not to deal with customers who can meet the usual trade terms offered by the supplier.

QUICK RECALL

I.   Name six marketing channels of distribution.

1. _____

2. _____

3. _____

4. _____

5. _____

6. _____

II.   Name three marketing channel functions performed by intermediaries.

1. _____

2. _____

3. _____

III. Name three types of transactional functions.

1. _____

2. _____

3. _____

IV.   Name four types of logistical functions.

1. _____

2. _____

3. _____

4. _____

V.   Name three types of facilitating functions.

1. _____

2. _____

3. _____

VI.   Name four utilities created by intermediaries.

1. _____

2. _____

3. _____

4. _____

VII. Name three types of wholesaling intermediaries.

1. _____

2. _____

3. _____

VIII. Name two types of merchant wholesalers.

1. _____

2. _____

IX.   Name two types of full-service wholesalers.

    1. _____

    2. _____

X.   Name four types of limited-service wholesalers.

    1. _____

    2. _____

    3. _____

    4. _____

XI.   Name two types of wholesaling agents.

    1. _____

    2. _____

XII.   Name three types of vertical marketing systems.

    1. _____

    2. _____

    3. _____

XIII.   Name four factors affecting channel choice and management.

    1. _____

    2. _____

    3. _____

    4. _____

XIV.   Name three important channel design considerations.

    1. _____

    2. _____

    3. _____

XV. Name at least five possible causes of conflict in marketing channels.

1. _____

2. _____

3. _____

4. _____

5. _____

XVI. Name six channel strategies or practices affected by legal restrictions.

1. _____

2. _____

3. _____

4. _____

5. _____

6. _____

TERMS AND DEFINITIONS

1. industrial distributor
2. direct channel
3. marketing channel
4. indirect channel
5. truck jobber
6. selling agents
7. general merchandise wholesalers
8. franchising
9. specialty merchandise wholesalers
10. channel captain
11. dual distribution
12. exclusive distribution
13. manufacturer's agent
14. selective distribution
15. brokers
16. intensive distribution
17. drop shipper
18. cash and carry wholesalers
19. Vertical marketing systems (VMS)
20. rack jobbers
21. direct marketing

DEFINING MARKETING CHANNELS OF DISTRIBUTION

1. retailer
2. dealer
3. middleman
4. wholesaler
5. distributor
6. agent or broker

RATIONALE FOR INTERMEDIARIES

1. facilitating
2. logistical
3. transactional
4. transactional
5. logistical
6. facilitating
7. facilitating
8. logistical
9. logistical
10. transactional

UTILITIES CREATED BY INTERMEDIARIES

1. form
2. place
3. time
4. place
5. form
6. time
7. possession
8. possession

MERCHANT WHOLESALERS

I.
1. limited service
2. limited service
3. full service
4. limited service
5. limited service
6. full service

II.
1. general merchandise
2. specialty merchandise
3. drop shipper
4. cash and carry
5. truck jobber
6. rack jobber

AGENTS AND BROKERS

1. selling agents
2. brokers
3. manufacturer's agents
4. manufacturer's agents
5. selling agents
6. brokers

MANUFACTURER'S BRANCHES AND OFFICES

I. 1. Wholly-owned extension of the manufacturer.
    2. Carries the manufacturer's inventory.
    3. Performs the functions of a full-service wholesaler.

II. 1. Wholly-owned extension of the manufacturer.
    2. Does not carry inventory.
    3. Performs only a selling function.

VERTICAL MARKETING SYSTEMS

I.   1. backward integration
     2. forward integration
     3. backward integration
     4. forward integration

II. Corporate systems represent an ownership interest; in administered
    systems, channel relationships and coordination are based on size,
    influence, and power.

III. 1. franchising
     2. retailer-sponsored cooperative
     3. wholesaler-sponsored voluntary chain
     4. franchising

FACTORS AFFECTING CHANNEL CHOICE AND MANAGEMENT

1. consumer factors
2. product factors
3. company factors
4. environmental factors

CHANNEL DESIGN CONSIDERATIONS

1. exclusive
2. intensive
3. selective
4. exclusive
5. selective
6. intensive

CHANNEL DESIGN CONSIDERATIONS

1. target market coverage
2. satisfying buyer requirements
3. profitability

CHANNEL RELATIONSHIPS

1. vertical conflict
2. horizontal conflict
3. vertical conflict
4. horizontal conflict

CHANNEL STRATEGIES AND PRACTICES AFFECTED BY LEGAL RESTRICTIONS

1. dual distribution
2. vertical integration
3. exclusive dealing
4. tying arrangements
5. resale restrictions
6. refusal to deal

QUICK RECALL

I. 1. retailer
    2. dealer
    3. middleman
    4. wholesaler
    5. distributor
    6. agent or broker

II. 1. transactional
    2. logistical
    3. facilitating

III. 1. buying
     2. selling
     3. risk taking

IV. 1. assorting
    2. storing
    3. sorting
    4. transporting

V. 1. financing
    2. grading
    3. marketing information and research

VI. 1. time
    2. place
    3. form
    4. possession

VII. 1. merchant wholesalers
     2. agents or brokers
     3. manufacturers branches and offices

VIII. 1. full-service wholesaler
      2. limited-service wholesaler

IX. 1. general merchandise
    2. specialty merchandise

X. 1. cash and carry
    2. drop shipper
    3. truck jobbers
    4. rack jobber

XI. 1. manufacturer's agents
    2. selling agents

XII. 1. corporate
     2. administered
     3. contractual

XIII.   1. product factors
        2. company factors
        3. environmental factors
        4. consumer factors

XIV.   1. target market coverage
        2. satisfying buyer requirements
        3. profitability

XV.   1. terms of sale
        2. promotion
        3. delivery
        4. territorial infringement
        5. preferential treatment

XVI.   1. vertical integration
        2. refusal to deal
        3. tying arrangements
        4. dual distribution
        5. resale restrictions
        6. exclusive dealing

14

PHYSICAL DISTRIBUTION AND LOGISTICS

TERMS AND DEFINITIONS

Listed below are the definitions of important physical distribution terms. Choose the correct term for each definition from the list below, and write it in the space provided.

Automated warehouse
Bonded warehouses
Business logistics
Customer service
Distribution centers
Freight forwarders
Intermodal transportation
Just-in-time concept

Lead time
Materials handling
Order cycle time
Physical distribution management
Public warehouse
Replenishment time
Shipper's associations
Total cost

1. _____ A narrow view of the distribution process which focuses on the flow of finished goods to the consumer, but does not include procuring or moving raw materials.

2. _____ The sum of all applicable costs for logistical activities.

3. _____ Computer-controlled technologies which replace people with machines in warehouses, cut labour costs, reduce loss and damage, improve safety, and provide better inventory record keeping.

4. _____ The ability of a logistics system to satisfy users in terms of time, dependability, communications and convenience.

5. _____ The time required to transmit, process, prepare, and ship an order, from the seller's viewpoint.

6. _____ A strategy for reducing inventories by using suppliers who can guarantee fast, reliable delivery of supplies to prevent production shutdowns.

7. _____ A type of privately-owned warehouse which specializes in the rapid movement of goods through the warehouse.

8. _____ The movement of small amounts of goods over short distances in supporting warehouse operations.

9. _____ Firms that accumulate small shipments into larger lots, then hire a carrier to move them, usually at reduced rates due to large shipment size.

10. _____ A specialized public warehouse which allows a firm to defer taxes on stored items until they are released.

11. _____ A facility which provides space and miscellaneous services on a rental basis to more than one firm.

12. _____ A cooperative of freight forwarders formed by several shippers to take advantage of reduced costs and better service.

13. _____ The time required to transmit, process, prepare, and ship an order from the buyer's viewpoint.

14. _____ Coordinating or combining different transportation modes to take advantage of the best features of each, while minimizing the shortcomings.

15. _____ A comprehensive term which covers coordinating the physical movement and storage of parts, raw materials, and finished goods to minimize total cost for a given service level.

16. _____ The lag from ordering an item until it is received in stock.

RELATION TO MARKETING STRATEGY

". . . The best laid marketing strategies can fail if the logistics system doesn't support them. A product cannot be purchased if it is not on the shelf when the consumer attempts to buy it."

Logistical factors interact with the four elements of the marketing mix.

> Product
> Pricing
> Promotion
> Place

Match the correct mix element with the logistical consideration or statements listed below:

1. _____ This factor includes considerations of physical characteristics, packaging, and product differentiation.

2. _____ Advertising campaigns must be coordinated with the logistics system to assure product availability at the correct time.

3. _____ Trade promotions and contests for the sales force may create irregular demand.

4. _____ Weight/bulk relationships, weight/value relationships, and associated buying risks are important aspects of this factor.

5. _____ Special attention is placed on movement and storage.

6. _____ The size of purchase can be affected both by quantity discount purchases as well as volume transportation discounts.

7. _____ Terms of transfer for the product's title and responsibility for transfer may be determined by specific geographic pricing systems.

8. _____ Logistical problems in this area have resulted in the involvement of middlemen.

CUSTOMER SERVICE DEFINITION AND OBJECTIVES

"Customer service is the ability of a logistics system to satisfy users in terms of time, dependability, communications, and convenience."

There are four important facets of customer service objectives:

>Time
>Dependability
>Communication
>Convenience

Match the correct service objective to the statements or examples listed below:

1. _____A two-way link between buyer and seller that helps in monitoring services.

2. _____Since different customers have different needs, customer service should be flexible to accommodate these needs.

3. _____This includes consistent lead time (the period from order placement to delivery), safe delivery, and correct delivery.

4. _____Reduction of the order cycle time or replenishment time, depending on the viewpoint (seller or buyer).

TRANSPORTATION

"There are five basic modes of transportation: railroads, motor carriers, air carriers, pipelines, and water carriers. In addition, there are modal combinations involving two or more of the five basic modes."

"All can be evaluated on six basic service dimensions:"

>Cost
>Time
>Capability
>Dependability
>Accessibility
>Frequency

Evaluate each of the five basic modes of transportation using the six service dimensions listed above:

	Railroads	Motor Carriers	Air Carriers	Pipelines	Water Carriers
1. Cost	_____	_____	_____	_____	_____
2. Time	_____	_____	_____	_____	_____
3. Capability	_____	_____	_____	_____	_____
4. Dependability	_____	_____	_____	_____	_____
5. Accessibility	_____	_____	_____	_____	_____
6. Frequency	_____	_____	_____	_____	_____

WAREHOUSING AND MATERIALS HANDLING

"A variety of warehousing arrangements exist to serve various needs."

Two main forms of warehouses include:

Public warehouses
Private warehouses

1. _____ They provide space and miscellaneous services on a rental basis.

2. _____ Both fixed and variable costs are present for the user.

3. _____ There are no fixed costs, long term commitments, or ownership risks, and are run by people who know the warehouse business.

4. _____ These warehouses are especially useful when new geographic or test markets are entered, and product demand is uncertain.

5. _____ This method of warehousing is cheaper in the long run if it is used extensively.

6. _____ Additional services include filing monthly inventory status reports, preparing transportation documents, weighing, monitoring loss and damage from transportation, and assisting in claim filing for such errors.

7. _____ Conditions that generally favour this type of
warehouse include a large, stable volume of stock
moving through the warehouse, adequate financial
resources to make the purchase, available managerial
expertise, and a need for control of warehousing
operations or some specific capabilities.

8. _____ Bonded warehouses allow deferment of taxes on items
such as liquor and tobacco until the stocks are
released.

*Challenge - Other warehousing options include materials handling warehousing
and transit warehousing. Discuss the relative merits of materials handling
warehousing and transit warehousing. (Make sure you include automated
warehouses.)

INVENTORY MANAGEMENT

"The major problem in managing inventory is maintaining the delicate
balance between too little, and too much of it."

I.   List the six traditional reasons for carrying inventory:

1. _____

2. _____

3. _____

4. _____

5. _____

6. _____

"Specific inventory costs are often hard to detect because they are spread throughout the firm in production warehouses and decentralized warehouses."

Four common inventory costs include:

Capital costs
Inventory service costs
Storage costs
Risk costs

II. Match the type of cost to the statements below.

1. _____Warehousing space and materials handling.

2. _____Items such as insurance and taxes that are present in most provinces, sometimes at an expensive rate.

3. _____Possible loss, damage, pilferage, perishability, and obsolescence.

4. _____The opportunity costs resulting from tying up funds in inventory instead of using them in other more profitable investments.

INVENTORY STRATEGIES

"Several methods exist for improving inventory management."

Just-in-time (JIT) concept
ABC analysis

Match the correct inventory management method with statements listed below:

1. _____Suppliers must be able to provide fast, reliable supplies, otherwise there might be a production disruption for the buyer.

2. _____Canadian Tire uses its own trucks and CN Rail to supply its 400 stores nation-wide on a timely basis.

3. _____Items are designated by the letters of the alphabet and according to some standard such as sales volume. Customer service levels are then set for each category.

I. What are four marketing mix variables which strategically interact with logistical considerations?

    1. _____

    2. _____

    3. _____

    4. _____

II. What are four types of customer service objectives?

    1. _____

    2. _____

    3. _____

    4. _____

III. What are six service dimensions used to evaluate various modes of transportation?

    1. _____

    2. _____

    3. _____

    4. _____

    5. _____

    6. _____

IV. List five major forms of distribution transportation.

    1. _____

    2. _____

    3. _____

    4. _____

    5. _____

V. Name two alternate forms of warehousing.

1. _____

2. _____

VI. List six traditional reasons for carrying inventory.

1. _____

2. _____

3. _____

4. _____

5. _____

6. _____

VII. List two methods of improving inventory management.

1. _____

2. _____

TERMS AND DEFINITIONS

1. physical distribution management
2. total cost
3. automated warehouse
4. customer service
5. order cycle time
6. just-in-time concept
7. distribution center
8. materials handling
9. freight forwarders
10. bonded warehouse
11. public warehouse
12. shippers' association
13. replenishment time
14. intermodal transportation
15. business logistics
16. lead time

RELATION TO MARKETING STRATEGY

1. product
2. promotion
3. promotion
4. product
5. place
6. pricing
7. pricing
8. place

CUSTOMER SERVICE DEFINITION AND OBJECTIVES

1. communication
2. convenience
3. dependability
4. time

TRANSPORTATION

	Railroads	Motor Carriers	Air Carriers	Pipelines	Water Carriers
1. Cost	low	high	high	low	low
2. Time	sometimes slow	fast	fast	slow	slow
3. Capability	full	some limitations	limited	limited	full
4. Dependability	poor	high	high	high	high
5. Accessibility	high	high	high	low	low
6. Frequency	low	high	high	n/a	low

WAREHOUSING AND MATERIALS HANDLING

1. public
2. private
3. public
4. public
5. private
6. public
7. private
8. public

INVENTORY MANAGEMENT

I.   1. As a buffer against variations in supply and demand.
     2. To provide better customer service.
     3. To promote production efficiencies.
     4. As a hedge against potential price increases by suppliers.
     5. To take advantage of purchasing and transportation discounts.
     6. To protect the firm against contingencies such as strikes, shortages, etc.

II. 1. storage costs
     2. inventory service costs
     3. risk costs
     4. capital costs

INVENTORY STRATEGIES

1. Just-in-time concept
2. Just-in-time concept
3. ABC analysis

QUICK RECALL

I.   1. product
     2. pricing
     3. promotion
     4. place (distribution)

II. 1. time
     2. dependability
     3. communication
     4. convenience

III. 1. cost   4. dependability
     2. time   5. accessibility
     3. capability   6. frequency

IV. 1. railroads
     2. air carriers
     3. motor carriers
     4. pipelines
     5. water carriers

V.   1. public warehouse
     2. private warehouse

VI. 1. As a buffer against variations in supply and demand.
     2. To provide better customer service.
     3. To promote production efficiencies.
     4. As a hedge against potential price increases by suppliers.
     5. To take advantage of purchasing and transportation discounts.
     6. To protect the firm against contingencies such as strikes, shortages, etc.

VII. 1. Just-in-time concept
     2. ABC analysis

15

RETAILING

Listed below are the definitions of important retailing terms. Choose the correct term for each definition from the list below, and write it in the space provided.

Breadth of product line
Central business district
Community shopping center
Depth of product line
Form of ownership
Green revolution
Hypermarket
Intertype competition
Level of service
Merchandise line
Method of operation
Off-price retailing

Piggyback franchising
Regional centers
Retail life cycle
Retail positioning matrix
Retailing
Retailing mix
Scrambled merchandising
Shrinkage
Strip location
Universal product code
Wheel of retailing

1. _____ A retail site location which typically has one primary store and a relatively large number of smaller outlets and serves a population base of about 100,000.

2. _____ A store that carries a wide variety of different items.

3. _____ The distinction of who owns a retail outlet. The alternatives are independent, corporate chain, cooperative, or franchise.

4. _____ Competition between dissimilar types of retail outlets brought about by scrambled merchandising.

5. _____ A store that carries a large assortment of each item.

6. _____ The manner in which services are provided - how and where the customer purchases products.

7. _____ A framework for positioning retail outlets in terms of breadth of product line and value added.

8. _____ A term used by retailers to describe theft of merchandise by customers and employees.

9. _____ A number assigned to identify each product and represented by a series of bars of varying widths for scanning.

10. _____This distinguishes the degree of service provided by a retailer: self-service, limited-service, or full-service.

11. _____The oldest retail setting, the community's downtown area.

12. _____This refers to how many different types of products a store carries and in what assortment.

13. _____A process of growth and decline that retail outlets, like products, experience.

14. _____This refers to the selling of brand name merchandise at a lower-than-regular price.

15. _____The offering by a retailer of several unrelated product lines in a single store.

16. _____A cluster of stores which serve people who live within a five to ten minute drive in a population base of under 30,000.

17. _____The strategy components which a retailer offers, including: (1) goods and services, (2) physical distribution, and (3) communications.

18. _____Suburban malls of today containing up to 100 stores.

19. _____All activities in selling, renting, and providing services to ultimate consumers for personal, and non-business use.

20. _____A description of how new forms of retail outlets enter the market and evolve over time, in terms of status and margin.

21. _____Large stores (over 100,000 square feet) which offer a mix of 40 percent food products and 60 percent general merchandise items.

22. _____Stores operated by one chain that sell the products of another franchise firm.

23. _____Canadian consumers are more conscious of their environment and will switch to retailers who offer environment friendly products.

CONSUMER UTILITIES OFFERED BY RETAILING

"Retailing provides multiple values to the consumer, these values are in the form of services provided, or utilities."

There are four consumer utilities:

Time
Place
Possession
Form

Match the type of utility with the examples or statements below:

1. _____ Tupperware, one of the largest direct sales companies, gives product demonstrations in customers' homes and delivers the customer orders, sorted and bagged, directly to the party hostess.

2. _____ A diner in a college town stays open 24 hours a day to cater to students who study late and factory workers who work second shift.

3. _____ A sewing machine retailer offers five free sewing lessons with the purchase of a new machine.

4. _____ A car dealer guarantees a $1,000 trade-in on your old car, regardless of its condition, when applied towards the purchase of a new car.

FORM OF OWNERSHIP

"One type of classification of retail outlets is form of ownership."

There are five different forms of ownership:

> Independent
> Corporate chain
> Consumer cooperative
> Trade cooperative
> Franchising

Match the correct form of ownership to the examples or statements listed below:

1. _____This form of ownership consists of multiple outlets under common ownership.

2. _____This form of ownership is an outlet owned by a group of consumers who also manage, operate, and shop at the store.

3. _____This form of ownership consists of independently-owned stores banding together to act like a chain. They may be either retail-sponsored or wholesale-sponsored.

4. _____One of the most common forms of retail ownership is ownership by an individual.

5. _____In this form of ownership, an individual or firm contracts with a parent company to set up a business or retail outlet.

LEVEL OF SERVICE

"Even though most customers perceive little variation in retail outlets by form of ownership, differences in retailers are more obvious when compared by level of service."

There are three levels of service classifications:

> Self-service
> Limited-service
> Full-service

Match the correct level of service with the examples or statements below:

1. _____ The Food Barn grocery store offers a full line of grocery products. However, merchandise is displayed in its original shipping packages (cardboard boxes) rather than in fancy displays, and customers box, bag, and carry their own groceries.

2. _____ A furniture store carries a broad line of high quality furniture. They also provide personal financing, free delivery, and free interior decorating services when you make a purchase.

3. _____ A department store carries a broad selection of small kitchen appliances in their housewares department. They have an informed sales staff, and will gladly gift wrap your purchases. However, they do not have a shop for repairs should your appliance need work after a long period of regular use.

*Challenge - Make a list of retail stores in your neighborhood. Find at least five for each level of service category. If it is more difficult to find stores in one category than in another, try to figure out why.

MERCHANDISE LINE

"Retail outlets also vary by their merchandise lines, the key distinction being the breadth and depth of the items offered to customers."

There are three merchandise line classifications:

General merchandise
Limited line
Scrambled merchandise

I.   Match the correct merchandise line classification with the statements or examples listed below:

1. _____Stores that carry a considerable assortment (depth) of a related line of items, or, stores that carry extraordinary depth in one primary line of merchandise.

2. _____Stores that offer several unrelated product lines in a single store.

3. _____Stores that carry a broad product line, with limited depth.

II. Find an example of a general merchandise, limited line, and scrambled merchandise store for each of the following products:

Example:	General Merchandise	Limited Line	Scrambled Merchandise
Shoes	Payless Shoe	The Foot Locker	K-Mart
1. Doughnuts	_____	_____	_____
2. Bicycles	_____	_____	_____

"Retail stores have begun to vary widely in the way their services are provided or the method of their operation."

"Classifying retail outlets by method of operation means dividing these outlets into store and non-store retailing."

There are five non-store methods of retailing operation:

Mail
In-home
Vending machine
Computer assisted
Television home shopping

I.   Make a list of at least five mail order catalogues. Record where these catalogues were advertised and how they can be obtained.

Example: DAMART

_____

_____

_____

_____

_____

_____

_____

II. Make a list of as many in-home retailers as you can find. Contact at least three to find out what special benefits are available to the host, hostess, or home consumer.

Example: Mary Kay Cosmetics

_____

_____

_____

_____

_____

III.   "Typically, small convenience products are available in vending machines, but with improved technology, larger, more expensive items are being sold in machines."

Make a list of at least 20 different <u>types</u> of products that are being sold in vending machines. Example: cigarette lighters

_____	_____
_____	_____
_____	_____
_____	_____
_____	_____
_____	_____
_____	_____
_____	_____
_____	_____
_____	_____

*Challenge - Check your newspaper to see if there is a home shopping network in your local area. If there is, watch it and make a list of the variety of items sold. Determine how the prices compare with similar items sold in traditional retail outlets.

RETAILING MIX

"In developing retail strategy, managers work with the retailing mix which includes: (1) goods and services, (2) physical distribution and (3) communications. Decisions relating to the mix focus on the consumer."

There are three basic areas of importance:

> Pricing
> Store location
> Image

Retail Pricing

I.   A retailer purchased an order of brass candlesticks. The price he paid per pair was $30.00. He first offered them for sale to his customers for $60.00 per pair. Although before the holidays the candlesticks sold well, by February they were hardly selling at all. He reduced the price to $45.00.

Using the above information determine:

1. original mark-up   _____

2. mark-down   _____

3. maintained mark-up   _____

*Challenge - "A new trend having a dramatic impact in retail pricing, commonly found in clothing sales, involves regularly selling name brand merchandise at lower than regular prices."

Visit an off-price retailer. Compare lowered prices to the original and determine the percentage of savings for the consumer. Discuss factors that could possibly counteract these savings. Try to find the location of the closest warehouse club.

Store Location

II. "Most stores today are near several others in one of four settings . . ."

> Central business district
> Community shopping center
> The Regional center
> A Strip location

Using the community in which you live or attend school as an example, identify stores in the four types of locations listed above. If all the areas are not represented, explain why.

_____

_____

_____

_____

*Challenge - Many small but growing towns are currently involved in controversies concerning the construction of Regional Centers (Shopping Malls). People fear malls will lead to the death of the Central Business Districts. Research and present the pro's and con's for each side.

Retail Image and Atmosphere

III. Make a list of those factors which contribute to a store's image and atmosphere. Visit a store that has a high prestige orientation and a store that has a casual and fun orientation. Compare use of lighting, colour, music, etc., for each store. Note also the type of clientele in each store. What conclusions can you draw from your comparison?

RETAIL LIFE CYCLE

There are four stages in the retail life cycle:

Early growth
Accelerated development
Maturity
Decline

Each stage in the retail life cycle suggests a different marketing strategy. Discuss likely marketing strategies for a retail store during each stage in the retail life cycle.

1. Early growth -_____

_____

2. Accelerated development -_____

_____

3. Maturity -_____

_____

4. Decline -_____

_____

FUTURE CHALLENGES IN RETAILING

*Challenge - Make a list of the different types of stores that are currently using UPCs to record sales.

_____

_____

_____

_____

Shrinkage problems are growing at an alarming rate. To see how accurate this statement is, devise an anonymous questionnaire for administration to your own class. Determine the average cost of a pilfered item and project the total loss from shrinkage for 100 people.

I.   What are five forms-of-ownership classifications for retail outlets?

      1. _____

      2. _____

      3. _____

      4. _____

      5. _____

II.   What are three level-of-service classifications for retail outlets?

      1. _____

      2. _____

      3. _____

III.   What are three merchandise classifications for retail outlets?

      1. _____

      2. _____

      3. _____

IV.   What are two method-of-operation classifications for retail outlets?

      1. _____

      2. _____

V.   List five types of non-store retailing.

      1. _____

      2. _____

      3. _____

      4. _____

      5. _____

VI. What are the two evaluated dimensions on a retail positioning matrix?

1. _____

2. _____

VII. Name three major elements of the retailing mix.

1. _____

2. _____

3. _____

VIII. List four settings (locations) where you will find most retail stores today.

1. _____

2. _____

3. _____

4. _____

IX. What are the four stages of the retail life cycle?

1. _____

2. _____

3. _____

4. _____

X. What are the four of the primary challenges facing retailers today?

1. _____

2. _____

3. _____

4. _____

TERMS AND DEFINITIONS

1. community shopping center
2. breadth of line
3. form of ownership
4. intertype competition
5. depth of line
6. method of operation
7. retail positioning matrix
8. shrinkage
9. universal product code
10. level of service
11. central business district
12. merchandise line
13. retail life cycle
14. off-price retailing
15. scrambled merchandising
16. strip location
17. retailing mix
18. regional centers
19. utilities
20. wheel of retailing
21. hypermarket
22. piggyback franchising

CONSUMER UTILITIES OFFERED BY RETAILING

1. place
2. time
3. form
4. possession

FORM OF OWNERSHIP

1. corporate chain
2. consumer cooperative
3. trade cooperative
4. independent
5. franchising

LEVEL OF SERVICE

1. self-service
2. full-service
3. limited-service

MERCHANDISE LINE

I. 1. limited line
    2. scrambled merchandise
    3. general merchandise

II. There are many possible answers. For further guidance refer to your text page(s): 415.

METHOD OF OPERATION

I.   There are many possible correct answers. For further guidance refer to your text page(s): 415-418.
1. L. L. Bean
2. Sears

II. There are many possible correct answers. For further guidance refer to your text page(s): 416-418.
1. Avon
2. Tupperware

III. There are many possible correct answers. For further guidance refer to your text page(s): 416-418.

RETAILING MIX

I.   Retail pricing
1. original mark-up: $60 - $30 = $30, or $30/$60 = 50%
2. mark-down: $60 - $45 = $15
3. maintained mark-up: $45 - $30 = $15, or $15/$45 = 33 1/3%

II. Store location - There are many possible correct answers. For further guidance refer to your text page(s): 422-423.

III. Retail image and atmosphere - There are many possible correct answers. For further guidance refer to your text page(s): 423-424.

RETAIL LIFE CYCLE

There are many possible answers. For further guidance refer to your text page(s): 425-426.

QUICK RECALL

I.   1. independent
2. corporate chain
3. consumer cooperative
4. trade cooperative
5. franchise

II. 1. self-service
2. limited-service
3. full-service

III. 1. general merchandise
2. limited line or single line
3. scrambled merchandising

IV. 1. store
2. non-store

V.   1. mail
       2. in-home
       3. vending machine
       4. computer assisted
       5. television home shopping

VI.   1. breadth of product line
       2. value added (service level and method of operation)

VII.   1. goods and services
       2. physical distribution
       3. communications

VIII. 1. central business district
       2. community shopping center
       3. regional shopping center
       4. a strip

IX.   1. early growth
       2. accelerated development
       3. maturity
       4. decline

X.   1. computerization
       2. the cost of shrinkage
       3. the green revolution
       4. the retailing of services

16

PROMOTIONAL PROCESS, SALES PROMOTION, AND PUBLICITY

Listed below are the definitions of important marketing terms. Choose the correct term for each definition from the list below, and write it in the space provided.

Advertising
Cause-related marketing
Communication
Consumer oriented sales promotions
    (consumer promotions)
Cooperative advertising
Decoding
Encoding
Feedback
Field of experience
Message

Personal selling
Promotional mix
Publicity
Publicity tools
Pull strategy
Push strategy
Receivers
Sales promotion
Source
Trade oriented sales promotions
            (trade promotions)

1. _____ A company or person who sends a message; an essential element in communication.

2. _____ Directing the promotional mix at channel members or intermediaries to gain their cooperation in ordering and stocking a product.

3. _____ Any paid form of interpersonal presentation of goods and services.

4. _____ Consumers who read, hear, or see the message.

5. _____ The process of having the sender transform an abstract idea into a set of symbols.

6. _____ A person's understanding and knowledge.

7. _____ Sales tools to support a company's advertising and personal selling efforts directed to ultimate consumers. Examples include coupons, sweepstakes and trading stamps.

8. _____ The information component of communication, sent by a source to a receiver.

9. _____ Any paid form of nonpersonal communication about an organization, product, or service by an identified sponsor.

10. _____ The sharing of meaning which requires five elements: a source, message, receiver, and process of encoding and decoding.

11. _____ The reverse process of having the receiver take a set of symbols, the message, and transform them back to an abstract idea.

12. _____ Closes the communication flow from receiver back to sender indicating whether the message was decoded and understood as intended.

13. _____ Directing the promotional mix at ultimate consumers in an attempt to get them to ask the retailer for the product.

14. _____ Sales tools used to support a company's advertising and personal selling efforts with channel members.

15. _____ The combination of alternatives that a company uses to communicate with consumers about its products. Alternatives include advertising, personal selling, publicity, and sales promotion.

16. _____ A nonpersonal, indirectly paid presentation of an organization, product, or service.

17. _____ Short-term inducement of value offered to arouse interest in buying a good or service.

18. _____ Methods used to get a nonpersonal, indirectly paid presentation of a company or its products. Examples are news releases, news conferences, and public service announcements.

19. _____ Programs by which a manufacturer pays a percentage of a retailer's local advertising expense for advertising the manufacturer's products.

20. _____ When the charitable contributions of a firm are tied directly to the customer revenues produced through the promotion of one of its products.

THE COMMUNICATION PROCESS

I.   List the five elements required for communication to occur.

1. _____

2. _____

3. _____

4. _____

5. _____

II. Choose two advertisements for rival products. Example: Coke/Pepsi, Bounty/Viva paper towels, etc. Identify the five elements of communication for each. Try to remain as "neutral" as possible and choose which advertisement promotes its product more effectively. Give reasons for your decision.

PROMOTIONAL MIX

A company can communicate with consumers by using one or more of four promotional alternatives:

Advertising
Personal selling
Publicity
Sales promotion

I.   Identify which of the four methods of promotion is being used in the examples listed below:

1. _____ Siskel and Ebert critique current motion pictures. Their evaluation of a movie can have a significant effect on box office sales.

2. _____ Tupperware dealers do product demonstrations in homes. They sell new products, replace broken products, and give personal advice on kitchen organization. Consumer feedback through dealers has resulted in many new and innovative product ideas.

3. _____ Toyota Motor Sales purchased a full-page colour advertisement in Business Week Magazine to promote its 1985 Family Camry.

4. _____ Colgate Palmolive mailed samples of its Ajax Dishwashing Liquid along with a 25 cent store coupon.

II. List advantages and disadvantages for each of the four promotional elements.

	Advantages	Disadvantages
1. Advertising	_____	_____
	_____	_____
	_____	_____
2. Personal selling	_____	_____
	_____	_____
	_____	_____
3. Publicity	_____	_____
	_____	_____
	_____	_____
4. Sales promotion	_____	_____
	_____	_____
	_____	_____

*Challenge - Try to find an example of a product which is currently being promoted with all four elements.

SELECTING PROMOTIONAL TOOLS

"In putting together the promotional mix, a marketer must consider the balance of elements to use."

I.   List five important factors which can affect the relative emphasis of promotional mix elements.

1. _____

2. _____

3. _____

4. _____

5. _____

II. The method of promotion often depends on the nature of the target market.

Choose two target markets you think would be receptive to the following promotional forms.

Advertising   1. _____

                  2. _____

Personal selling 3. _____

                  4. _____

Publicity   5. _____

                  6. _____

Sales promotion   7. _____

                  8. _____

PRODUCT LIFE CYCLE

"The composition of the promotional mix changes over the four product life cycle stages."

I.   In which stage in the product life cycle would you expect to find the following objectives?

            Introduction
            Growth
            Maturity
            Decline

1. _____Gain brand preference and solidify distribution.

2. _____Increase the level of consumer awareness.

3. _____Maintain existing buyers, encourage brand loyalty.

4. _____Few promotional objectives; little money is spent on the promotional mix.

II. During which stage in the product life cycle would you expect the relative emphasis of the promotional mix elements to be as follows:

1. _____ Sales promotion is less, publicity is not a factor, the major promotional element is advertising, which stresses brand differences, personal selling is used to solidify the channel of distribution.

2. _____ Usually a period of phase-out and little money is spent on any element of the promotional mix.

3. _____ Advertising's role is reduced to reminding buyers of the product's existence. Sales promotion in the form of discounts and coupons are offered to both ultimate consumers and intermediaries. Sales force maintains satisfaction of intermediaries.

4. _____ All promotional elements are stressed, trial samples may be sent, sales force approaches new intermediaries.

PRODUCT CHARACTERISTICS

In designing the proper blend of elements in the promotional mix, companies consider three product characteristics, complexity, degree of risk, and ancillary services.

For each of the characteristics listed below, state whether the promotional emphasis would be towards (1) personal selling or (2) advertising.

1. _____ A relatively complex product like a VAX minicomputer.

2. _____ A product with little social, physical, or monetary risk, such as Bayer aspirin.

3. _____ A statistical software program which features sales, technical, and service support.

CUSTOMER'S STAGE OF DECISION MAKING

"Knowing the customer's stage in decision making can also affect the promotional mix."

There are three stages in a consumer's purchase decision:

> Pre-purchase stage
> Purchase stage
> Post-purchase stage

At which stage in the consumer purchase decision would the following statements hold true:

1. _____ The importance of personal selling is highest and the impact of advertising is lowest. Sales promotion in the form of price discounts can be very helpful.

2. _____ Advertising and personal selling help reduce the buyer's feelings of anxiety. Sales promotion in the form of coupons can help encourage repeat purchases.

3. _____ Advertising is more helpful than personal selling. Sales promotion in the form of free samples encourages low-risk trial.

*Challenge - Explain the significant similarities and differences between the push strategy and pull strategy.

SELECTING PROMOTIONAL TOOLS

In which of the following situations would you emphasize advertising, and in which situations would you emphasize personal selling?

1. _____ pull channel strategy

2. _____ great geographic dispersion of customers

3. _____ high level of ancillary services

4. _____ customers in the purchase stage of purchase decision

5. _____ product simple to understand

6. _____ small DMU (Decision Making Unit)

7. _____ push channel strategy

8. _____ complex product

9. _____ large DMU (Decision Making Unit)

10. _____ ultimate consumer is target market

11. _____ low purchase risk

12. _____ geographic concentration of customers

13. _____ target market of resellers and industrial buyers

14. _____ high risk in purchase

15. _____ pre-purchase stage of purchase decision

16. _____ low level of ancillary services

SALES PROMOTION

I.   From an historical perspective, list four possible sales promotion objectives.

1. _____

2. _____

3. _____

4. _____

II. There are numerous sales promotion alternatives. The text discusses:

Coupons
Deals
Premiums
Contests
Sweepstakes

Samples
Trading stamps
Point-or-purchase displays
Rebates

Match the form of sales promotion to the statements below:

1. _____ Buy one dinner, get a second dinner of equal or lower value, for half price.

2. _____ Try your skill at creating a new recipe using our crisp new crackers, and you may win a beautiful fully-equipped kitchen.

3. _____ Just rub off the magic seal and see if you are an instant winner.

4. _____ Send in five box tops and 50 cents postage and handling to receive your beautiful colour poster of Michael Jackson.

5. _____ Receive free stamps with every gasoline purchase. Stamps may be redeemed for valuable gifts.

6. _____Please try these new local cookies with our compliments.

7. _____Retailers, these new lollipops come with their own attractive free-standing carousel that fits perfectly next to your cash register.

8. _____Mail in three UPCs and cash register tapes with the price circled to receive a check for the full purchase price.

9. _____Receive 25 cents off your next purchase of McCain frozen peas for redeeming this.

*Challenge - Why do you think a point-of-purchase display with no reduced price might generate more sales than a reduced price with no special display?

TRADE-ORIENTED SALES PROMOTIONS

Trade-oriented sales promotions supplement advertising and personal selling and are directed to wholesalers, retailers, or distributors.

There are three types of trade-oriented sales promotions:

    Merchandise allowances
    Case allowances
    Finance allowances

I. Match the type of trade-oriented sales promotion with the examples or statements below:

1. _____This reimburses a retailer for extra in-store support or special featuring of the brand.

2. _____Manufacturers allow discounts on each case ordered during a specific time period.

3. _____Retailers may receive some amount of the product free, based on the amount ordered.

4. _____Retailers are paid for financing costs or financial losses associated with consumer sales promotions.

5. _____Retailers are given allowances that compensate them for transporting orders from the manufacturer's warehouse.

*Challenge - What are possible disadvantages of using trade-oriented sales promotions?

*CHALLENGE- "Resellers often perform the important function of promoting manufacturer's products at the local level."

Try to find examples of cooperative advertising in your local newspaper.

*CHALLENGE- "A manufacturer's success often rests on the ability or the reseller's sales force to represent its products. So it is in the best interest of the manufacturer to help train the reseller's sales forces."

Contact local firms, and supermarkets to determine to what degree manufacturers participate in the training of local reseller personnel.

PUBLICITY

"Publicity is a nonpersonal indirectly paid form of personal presentation of an organization, product, or service."

I. Three publicity tools that are available to the public relations director are:

> News releases
> News conferences
> Public service announcements

Find two current examples of each of the above-mentioned publicity tools.

_____

_____

_____

_____

Cause-related marketing is when the charitable contributions of a firm are tied directly to the customer revenues produced through the promotion of one of its products.

II. Find two examples of cause-related marketing. Find out what percentage of consumer sales actually goes to the selected "cause." Also, if possible, find the total yearly net profit contributed.

_____

_____

_____

_____

ETHICAL DIMENSIONS OF PROMOTION IN TODAY'S SOCIETY

*CHALLENGE- In recent years there has been growing concern in the area of promotion regarding:

> Misleading sale promotions and advertisements
> Advertising and TV programs directed toward children
> Realistic portrayals of women and minorities

Find at least one current example of each.

QUICK RECALL

I. What are five elements required for communication?

1. _____
2. _____
3. _____
4. _____
5. _____

II. What are the four elements of the promotional mix?

1. _____
2. _____
3. _____
4. _____

III. List five important factors which can affect the promotional mix.

1. _____
2. _____
3. _____
4. _____
5. _____

IV. List nine possible sales promotion alternatives.

1. _____   6. _____

2. _____   7. _____

3. _____   8. _____

4. _____   9. _____

5. _____

V. What are three types of trade-oriented sales promotions?

1. _____

2. _____

3. _____

VI. What are three publicity tools available to the public relations director?

1. _____

2. _____

3. _____

VII. List three major ethical concerns regarding promotional activities.

1. _____

2. _____

3. _____

TERMS AND DEFINITIONS

1. source
2. push strategy
3. personal selling
4. receivers
5. encoding
6. field of experience
7. consumer-oriented sales promotions (consumer promotions)
8. message
9. advertising
10. communication
11. decoding
12. feedback
13. pull strategy
14. trade-oriented sales (trade promotions)
15. promotional mix
16. publicity
17. sales promotions
18. publicity tools
19. cooperative advertising
20. cause-related marketing

THE COMMUNICATION PROCESS

I. 1. source
   2. encoding
   3. message
   4. decoding
   5. receivers

II. There are many possible correct answers. For further guidance refer to your text page(s): 437-438.

PROMOTIONAL MIX

I. 1. publicity
   2. personal selling
   3. advertising
   4. sales promotion

II.

	Advantages	Disadvantages
1. Advertising	Message control Can target the market	Cost Lack of direct feedback
2. Personal selling	Message control Absolute target market control Direct and immediate feedback	Cost Inconsistency in communications
3. Publicity	Credibility Only an indirect cost	No message control No timing control No target market control

	Advantages	Disadvantages
4. Sales promotion	Stimulates sales Can generate consumer interest Encourages promotional support	Some aspects are regulated Effect is temporary Timing is crucial

SELECTING PROMOTIONAL TOOLS

I. 1. stage of the product's life cycle
    2. target audience
    3. product characteristics
    4. buyer decision stage
    5. channel of distribution

II. Advertising
        1. teens - soft drinks
        2. yuppies - example: wine coolers, Volvo's, etc.
    Personal selling
        3. industrial buyers - example: fasteners
        4. housewives with children - example: cutlery
    Publicity
        5. the elderly - example: insurance, investments
        6. concerned parents - example: food nutrition, child care
    Sales promotion
        7. reluctant dealers - example: free goods
        8. consumers who believe their chances to win in the Reader's Digest Sweepstakes increases for each additional subscription placed

PRODUCT LIFE CYCLE

I. 1. growth
    2. introduction
    3. maturity
    4. decline

II. 1. growth
    2. decline
    3. maturity
    4. introduction

PRODUCT CHARACTERISTICS

1. personal selling
2. advertising
3. personal selling

CUSTOMER'S STAGE OF DECISION MAKING

1. purchase stage
2. post-purchase stage
3. pre-purchase stage

16-14

SELECTING PROMOTIONAL TOOLS

1. advertising
2. advertising
3. personal selling
4. personal selling
5. advertising
6. advertising
7. personal selling
8. personal selling
9. personal selling
10. advertising
11. advertising
12. personal selling
13. personal selling
14. personal selling
15. advertising
16. advertising

SALES PROMOTION

I.
1. Encourage new product trial.
2. Increase business inventory.
3. Increase repeat purchases.
4. Reduce price cutting.

II.
1. deals
2. contests
3. sweepstakes
4. premiums (self-liquidating)
5. trading stamps
6. samples
7. point-of-purchase displays
8. rebates
9. coupons

TRADE-ORIENTED SALES PROMOTIONS

1. merchandise allowance
2. case allowance
3. case allowance (free goods)
4. finance allowance
5. finance allowance (freight allowance)

PUBLICITY

I. & II. There are many possible correct answers. For further guidance refer to your text page(s): 456-457.

ETHICAL DIMENSIONS OF PROMOTIONS IN TODAY'S SOCIETY

There are many possible correct answers. For further guidance refer to your text page(s): 458.

QUICK RECALL

I.
1. source
2. encoding
3. message
4. decoding
5. receivers

II. 1. personal selling
     2. advertising
     3. publicity
     4. sales promotion

III. 1. stage of the product's life cycle
     2. product characteristics
     3. buyer decision stage
     4. target market characteristics
     5. channel strategies

IV. 1. coupons   6. samples
     2. deals   7. trading stamps
     3. premiums   8. point-of-purchase display
     4. contests   9. rebates
     5. sweepstakes

V.   1. allowances and discounts
     2. cooperative advertising
     3. training of distributors' salesforce

VI. 1. news releases
     2. news conferences
     3. public service announcements

VII. 1. misleading sales promotions and advertisements
     2. advertising and TV programs directed toward children
     3. realistic portrayals of woman and minorities

17

ADVERTISING

Listed below are the definitions of important marketing terms. Choose the correct term for each definition from the list below, and write it in the space provided.

Advertising
All you can afford budgeting
Competitive parity budgeting
Cost per thousand (CPM)
Frequency
Full service agency
Gross rating points
Hierarchy of effects
In house agencies
Institutional advertisements

Limited service agencies
Objective and task budgeting
Percentage of sales budgeting
Post tests
Pretests
Product advertisements
Rating
Reach

1. _____ Advertisements which focus on selling a product or service and take three forms: (1) pioneering, (2) competitive, and (3) reminder.

2. _____ Funds allocated to advertising as a percentage of past sales, anticipated unit sales, or anticipated total sales.

3. _____ Funds allocated to advertising according to the desired objectives and the tasks necessary to accomplish these objectives.

4. _____ The number of different people exposed to the message.

5. _____ Tests conducted before an advertisement is placed to determine whether it communicates the intended message or to select between alternative versions of an advertisement.

6. _____ An advertising agency which specializes in one aspect of the advertising process, such as providing creative services to develop the advertising copy or buying previously unpurchased media space.

7. _____ The stages from initial awareness of a product to eventual action. The sequence is awareness, interest, evaluation, trial, and adoption.

8. _____ A unit in a company which is the company's own group of advertising people who are included on the company payroll.

9. _____ Advertising agencies providing a broad range of market research services, media selection, copy development, artwork, and production for clients.

10. _____ Any paid-for form of nonpersonal presentation of goods, ideas, or services by an identified sponsor.

11. _____ Advertisements designed to build goodwill or an image for an organization, rather than promote a specific product or service.

12. _____ Funds allocated to advertising to match competitors' levels of spending.

13. _____ How often the same people see an advertisement.

14. _____ The cost of reaching one thousand individuals or households with the advertising message in a given medium.

15. _____ Tests conducted after an advertisement is run in a medium to assess whether it accomplished its intended purpose.

16. _____ Funds allocated to advertising only after all other budget items are covered.

17. _____ The percentage of households in a market watching or listening to a broadcast.

PRODUCT ADVERTISING

Product advertising focuses on selling a product or service, and can take three forms:

Pioneering
Competitive
Reminder

Match the correct form of product advertising with the definitions or statements below:

1. _____ Advertising that promotes a specific brand's features and benefits.

2. _____ Advertising that tells what a product is, what it can do, and where it can be found.

3. _____ This form of advertisement is used to reinforce prior knowledge of a product or a service.

4. _____ This form of advertising is often used in the maturity stage of the product life cycle.

5. _____ This form of advertising is often used in the introduction stage of the product life cycle.

6. _____ Firms that use this type of advertising need market research and test results to provide legal support for their claims.

7. _____ A Volvo ad tells consumers that ". . . the Volvo motor car has had the best safety record over the last 20 years of any auto driven in America."

*Challenge - Comparative competitive advertising and reinforcement reminder advertising are two more important terms. Using print advertisements, find five examples for each.

INSTITUTIONAL ADVERTISING

There are three alternative forms of institutional advertising:

> Advocacy advertisements
> Pioneering institutional advertisements
> Competitive institutional advertisements
> Reminder institutional

Match the correct form of institutional advertising to the definitions or statements below:

1. _____ These advertisements are used for a new announcement such as what a company is, what it can do, or where it is located.

2. _____ These advertisements promote the advantages of one product class over another.

3. _____ These advertisements state the position of a company on a given issue.

4. _____ An announcement by IBM touting the company as ". . . your new telecommunications partner."

5. _____ Recycle aluminum cans to keep our country clean.

6. _____ Seagrams is currently featuring a "Don't Drive Drunk" campaign, primarily using outdoor advertising.

7. _____ These advertisements bring the name of the company to the attention of their target market.

THE FOUR Ws

The development of the advertising program focuses on the four Ws:

<u>Who</u> is the target audience?
<u>What</u> are (a) the advertising objectives, (b) the
amount of money that can be budgeted for the
advertising program, and (c) the kinds of copy
to use?
<u>When</u> should the advertisements be run?
<u>Where</u> should the advertisements be run?

You are in charge of advertising for a small cleaning firm in your university, city, or town. You specialize in cleaning private homes and business offices on a weekly, bi-weekly, or monthly basis. Your total marketing budget is $2,000. Ten percent of that is allotted to advertising. Use any real information based on local advertising media to answer all four "Ws." Develop your advertising program.

<u>Who</u>: _____

<u>What</u>: (1)_____

(2)_____

(3)_____

<u>When</u>: _____

<u>Where</u>: _____

*Challenge - Using the information in Figure 17-6 in your text, figure the Cost per thousand (CPM) for the local newspaper vs. local radio.

HIERARCHY OF EFFECTS

"After the target audience is identified, a decision must be reached on what the advertising campaign is to accomplish. Consumers can be said to respond in terms of a hierarchy of effects . . ."

Awareness
Interest
Evaluation
Trial
Adoption

I. Match the correct stage in the hierarchy of effects to the definitions below:

1. _____ Through a favorable experience on the first trial, the consumer's repeated purchase and use of the product or brand.

2. _____ Consumers' appraisal of how they feel about the product or brand.

3. _____ The consumer's actual first purchase and use of the product or brand.

4. _____ The consumer's ability to recognize and remember the product or brand name.

5. _____ An increase in the knowledge of the product or brand until he knows and likes some of its features.

II. Match the advertising objective to the level of hierarchy of effect.

Awareness
Interest
Evaluation
Trial
Adoption

1. _____ Within 30 days after our ad in Sunday magazine, have 10,000 customers call our toll-free number requesting life insurance information.

2. _____ Within three months have 75% of all restaurants in town know about our line of cleaning services.

3. _____ During the month of January have 50 women participate in a free workout at our spa.

4. _____ By 1992 have 15 percent of consumers rate this news program as the most informative.

5. _____ After two weeks of heavy advertising and five free newspapers to all non-subscribers on each route, have each news carrier gain an average of five new subscribers.

*Challenge - "The central element of advertising copy . . . usually involves identifying the principal features of the product that are deemed important to a prospective buyer in making trial and adoption decisions."

Choose a product that has well-known competitors. Write an ad using the information suggested in Chapter 17.

OR

*Challenge - There has been a great deal of controversy lately concerning advertising and children. Watch at least two hours of children's television on a weekend morning. List the elements that are used to persuade children to buy the products.

MESSAGE CONTENT

"Information and persuasive content can be combined in the form of an appeal to provide a basic reason for the consumer to act."

There are three commonly used methods of appeal:

> Fear appeal
> Sex appeal
> Humorous appeal

List two current examples of advertisements that incorporate each of the above listed forms of appeal.

_____

_____

_____

_____

_____

_____

SETTING THE ADVERTISING BUDGET

"After setting the advertising objectives, a company must decide on how much to spend."

There are several methods used to set the advertising budget:

> Percent of sales
> Competitive parity
> All you can afford
> Objective and task

I.   Match the method of setting the advertising budget to the examples or statements below:

1. _____ Our chief competitor is placing three full-page colour ads in Good Housekeeping magazine. We must direct enough funds through advertising to cover at least three full-page colour ads, if not more.

2. _____ Our gross sales last year were $300,000 and our anticipated sales for next year are $400,000. Let's budget our advertising based on 5 percent of the average of last year's sales and this year's anticipated sales, or $17,500.

3. _____ "How much money can we possibly allocate for advertising?" "Fine, then, that's what we need."

4. _____ We have to reach at least 75 percent of the commuters in a 50 mile radius. To do that we'll have to advertise on local radio between 6-8 a.m. and 4-6 p.m. This will cost us $3,700. If we can't afford full coverage we can cut the evening ads to one hour.

II. What are the advantages and disadvantages for each of the methods of setting advertising budgets?

	Advantages	Disadvantages
Percent of sales	1. _____ _____ _____	1. _____ _____ _____
Competitive parity	2. _____ _____ _____	2. _____ _____ _____
Affordable	3. _____ _____ _____	3. _____ _____ _____
Objective and task	4. _____ _____ _____	4. _____ _____ _____

SCHEDULING THE ADVERTISING

"Scheduling advertising involves striking a balance between reach and frequency."

The scheduling phase of the advertising decision process involves determining how often ads should be run and determining the number of people who should be exposed to the ads.

*Challenge - Call several newspapers to investigate reach and frequency. Given an imaginary budget of $5,000 and five insertions per week (weekdays), what is the greatest reach and frequency you can achieve in placing a standard one inch ad over a three week period?

TIMING

"Setting schedules requires an understanding of how the market behaves. Most companies tend to follow one of two basic approaches."

Steady "drip" schedule
Pulse "burst" schedule

1. _____ Advertising which is run at a regular schedule throughout the year when demand and seasonal factors are unimportant.

2. _____ A major card manufacturer runs a special ad campaign in the spring right before graduation.

3. _____ Advertising which is distributed unevenly throughout the year because of seasonal demand, heavy periods of promotion, or the introduction of a new product.

4. _____ The original "soap operas" were sponsored by soap manufacturers.

MEDIA SELECTION

"Every advertiser must decide where to place advertisements. This decision is related to the target audience, type of product, available budget, and campaign objectives."

Every type of media has its special advantages and drawbacks. List the advantages and disadvantages for each of the media forms listed below:

Advantages

Disadvantages

Television: 1. _____   1. _____

_____   _____

_____   _____

_____   _____

Radio: 2. _____   2. _____

_____   _____

_____   _____

_____   _____

Magazines: 3. _____   3. _____

                  _____   _____

                  _____   _____

                  _____   _____

Newspapers: 4. _____   4. _____

                  _____   _____

                  _____   _____

                  _____   _____

Direct Mail: 5. _____   5. _____

                  _____   _____

                  _____   _____

                  _____   _____

Billboards: 6. _____   6. _____

                  _____   _____

                  _____   _____

                  _____   _____

Transit: 7. _____   7. _____

                  _____   _____

                  _____   _____

                  _____   _____

Theater: 8. _____   8. _____

                  _____   _____

                  _____   _____

                  _____   _____

*Challenge - You have a small home-based business that makes old-fashioned wooden toys. Select a magazine that you feel will most accurately cover your target market. Find out how much an ad will cost for different sizes, frequencies, and durations.

*Challenge - There are many other forms of advertising media that were not discussed in this chapter. See how many additional forms of media you can find, for example: matchbook covers.

PRETESTING ADVERTISING

Pretesting is done to determine whether the advertisement communicates the intended message, or to select the best alternative version of an advertisement.

There are three common forms of pretesting:

> Portfolio tests
> Jury tests
> Theater tests

Match the correct form of pretesting with the statements below:

1._____This is used to test copy alternatives. The test ad is placed in a booklet with several others ads and stories. Subjects are asked to read through and give their impressions of the ad on several evaluative scales.

2._____The ad is shown to a panel of consumers: the panel rates how much they liked the ad, how much it drew their attention, how attractive it was, etc.

3._____This is the most sophisticated form of pretesting. Consumers are invited to view a new movie or television show. During the show, commercials are shown. Viewers register their feeling about the advertisements either on hand-held electronic recording devices used during the viewing or on questionnaires afterwards.

POSTTESTING METHODS

There are several posttesting methods:

>   Aided recall
>   Unaided recall
>   Attitude tests
>   Inquiry tests
>   Sales tests

Match the correct posttesting method to the statements below:

1._____ This technique questions respondents without any prompting to determine whether they saw or heard advertising messages.

2._____ This technique offers additional product information, samples, or premiums in response to consumer requests. Ads generating the most inquiries are presumed to be the most effective

3._____ After being shown an ad, respondents are asked whether their previous exposure to it was through reading, viewing, or listening.

4._____ This technique involves studies such as controlled media comparison experiments and consumer purchase tests.

5._____ Respondents are asked questions to measure changes in their dispositions towards a particular product following an advertising campaign.

QUICK RECALL

I. What are the three main forms of product advertising?

   1. _____

   2. _____

   3. _____

II. What are four main forms of institutional advertising?

   1. _____

   2. _____

   3. _____

   4. _____

III.   What are the 4 "W's"?

   1. _____

   2. _____

   3. _____

   4. _____

IV.   What are the five stages in the hierarchy of effects?

   1. _____

   2. _____

   3. _____

   4. _____

   5. _____

V.   What are three methods of appeal?

   1. _____

   2. _____

   3. _____

VI.   What are four common methods used to determine an advertising budget?

   1. _____

   2. _____

   3. _____

   4. _____

VII.   What are two approaches used in setting advertising schedules?

   1. _____

   2. _____

VIII. What are the eight major advertising media?

1. _____

2. _____

3. _____

4. _____

5. _____

6. _____

7. _____

8. _____

IX. What are the three common forms of pretesting?

1. _____

2. _____

3. _____

X. What are five popular forms of posttesting?

1. _____

2. _____

3. _____

4. _____

5. _____

TERMS AND DEFINITION

1. product advertisements
2. percent of sales budgeting
3. objective and task budgeting
4. reach
5. pretests
6. limited service agencies
7. hierarchy of effects
8. in-house agencies
9. full-service agencies

10. advertising
11. institutional advertisements
12. competitive parity
13. frequency
14. cost per thousand (cpm)
15. posttesting
16. all you can afford budgeting
17. rating

PRODUCT ADVERTISING

1. competitive
2. pioneering
3. reminder
4. reminder

5. pioneering
6. competitive (comparative)
7. reminder

INSTITUTIONAL ADVERTISING

1. pioneering institutional advertisements
2. competitive institutional advertisements
3. advocacy advertisements
4. pioneering institutional advertisements
5. competitive institutional advertisements
6. advocacy advertisements
7. reminder institutional advertisements

THE FOUR Ws

There are many possible correct answers. For further guidance refer to your text page(s): 469.

HIERARCHY OF EFFECTS

I. 1. adoption
    2. evaluation
    3. trial
    4. awareness
    5. interest

II. 1. interest
     2. awareness
     3. trial
     4. evaluation
     5. adoption

MESSAGE CONTENT

There are many possible correct answers. For further guidance refer to your text page(s): 474.

SETTING THE ADVERTISING BUDGET

I. 1. competitive parity
    2. percent of sales
    3. all you can afford
    4. objective and task

II.

	Advantages	Disadvantages
Percent of sales	1. Simple to use Advertising tied to sales	1. Causation fallacy Not related to objectives No logical basis for choosing a specific percentage
Competitive parity	2. Very simple to use Ensures parity in spending Prevents promotional "wars"	2. Assumes you have same objectives as competitors Assumes competition is spending at correct level
Affordable	3. Simple	3. No rationale for this approach
Objective & task	4. Incorporates objectives	4. Many judgmental inputs

TIMING

1. steady "drip" schedule
2. pulse "burst" schedule
3. pulse "burst" schedule
4. steady "drip" schedule

MEDIA SELECTION

	Advantages	Disadvantages
Television	1. Large audience reach More sensory stimulation High prestige	1. High cost Wasted coverage
Radio	2. Good target market selectivity Widely available Relatively low cost	2. Only audio effects Short message life
Magazines	3. Good target market selectivity Relatively long life Multiple readership Good reproduction	3. Relatively high cost Low frequency Relatively long lead times
Newspapers	4. Large audiences Short lead time Low relative cost Frequent publication	4. Poor reproduction Short life Little audience selectivity
Direct Mail	5. High selectivity More information conveyed	5. High waste Relatively expensive Sometimes viewed negatively
Billboards	6. Relatively low cost Good reach & frequency Geographic selectivity Good for awareness	6. Legal restrictions Message limitations Little demographic selectivity
Transit	7. Geographic selectivity Relatively low cost Relatively low cost Diverse audience	7. Little demographic selectivity Not a high impact medium
Theater	8. Captive audience Some audience selectivity	8. Sometimes viewed negatively

NOTE: You may find more advantages or disadvantages than listed.

PRETESTING ADVERTISING

1. portfolio tests
2. jury tests
3. theater tests

17-18

POSTTESTING METHODS

1. unaided recall
2. inquiry test
3. aided recall
4. sales tests
5. attitude tests

QUICK RECALL

I.   1. pioneering
     2. competitive
     3. reminder

II. 1. advocacy
     2. pioneering institutional
     3. competitive institutional
     4. reminder institutional

III. 1. Who is the target audience?
     2. What are (a) the advertising objectives, (b) the amount of money
        budget, and (c) the kinds of copy to use?
     3. When should the advertisements run?
     4. Where should the advertisements be run?

IV. 1. awareness
     2. interest
     3. evaluation
     4. trial
     5. adoption

V.   1. sex appeal
     2. humorous appeal
     3. fear appeal

VI. 1. competitive parity
     2. all you can afford
     3. percent of sales
     4. objective and task

VII. 1. steady "drip" schedule
     2. pulse "burst" schedule

VIII. 1. television
      2. radio
      3. magazines
      4. newspapers
      5. direct mail
      6. billboards
      7. transit
      8. theater

IX. 1. portfolio
     2. jury
     3. theater

X.   1. unaided recall
    2. inquiry tests
    3. aided recall
    4. sales tests
    5. attitude tests

18

PERSONAL SELLING AND SALES MANAGEMENT

TERMS AND DEFINITIONS

Listed below are the definitions of important personal selling terms. Choose the correct term for each definition from the list below, and write it in the space provided.

Account management policies
Combination compensation plan
Formula selling presentation
Job analysis
Missionary sales people
Needs-satisfaction presentation
Order getter
Order taker
Personal selling

Personal selling process
Sales engineer
Sales management
Sales plan
Stimulus-response presentation
Straight commission compensation
  plan
Straight salary compensation plan
Team selling
Work load method

1. _____ The practice of using a group of professionals with different areas of expertise in selling and servicing major customers.

2. _____ A statement describing what is to be achieved and where and how the selling effort of salespeople is to be deployed.

3. _____ A compensation plan in which the salesperson is paid a fixed amount per week, month, or year.

4. _____ A salesperson who sells in a conventional sense and engages in identifying prospective customers, providing customers with information, persuading customers to buy, closing sales, and following-up on customers' use of a product or service.

5. _____ Sales activities occurring before and after the sale itself, consists of six stages: (1) prospecting, (2) preapproach, (3) approach, (4) presentation, (5) close, and (6) follow-up.

6. _____ Policies that specify whom salespeople should contact, what kinds of selling and customer service activities should be engaged in, and how these activities should be carried out.

7. _____ A written description of what a salesperson is expected to do.

8. _____ A salesperson who processes routine orders and reorders products that are presold by the company.

9. _____ A selling formula that emphasizes probing and listening by salespeople to identify the needs and interests of prospective buyers.

10. _____ A formula-based method that integrates the number of customers served, call frequency, call length, and available selling time to arrive at a sales force size figure.

11. _____ A salesperson who specializes in identifying, analyzing, and solving customer problems and brings know-how and technical expertise to the selling situation, but often does not actually sell products and services.

12. _____ A selling format that assumes if given the appropriate stimulus by the salesperson, the prospect will buy.

13. _____ The planning, implementing, and controlling of the personal selling effort of the firm.

14. _____ A compensation plan in which a salesperson's earnings are directly tied to his or her sales or profits generated.

15. _____ The two-way flow of communication between buyer and seller that often occurs in a face-to-face encounter, designed to influence a person's or group's purchase decision.

16. _____ A selling format that assumes a presentation consists of information that must be provided in an accurate, thorough, and step-by-step manner to persuade the prospect to buy.

17. _____ A compensation plan in which a salesperson is paid a specified salary plus a commission and/or bonus on sales or profits generated.

18. _____ Sales support personnel who do not directly solicit orders but rather concentrate on performing promotional activities and introducing new products.

COMPARING ORDER-TAKERS AND ORDER-GETTERS

Which of the following activities are performed by order-takers, and which are performed by order-getters?

1. _____Handles routine product orders and/or reorders.

2. _____Generates new sales volume.

3. _____Identifies new customers and sales opportunities.

4. _____Maintains sales volume.

5. _____Represents simple products with few options.

6. _____Requires significant sales training.

7. _____Focuses on straight rebuy purchase situations.

8. _____Requires significant clerical training.

9. _____Performs order processing functions.

10._____Acts as a creative problem solver.

11._____Focuses on new buy and modified rebuy purchase situations.

12._____Represents complex products with many options.

SALES SUPPORT PERSONNEL

"Sales support personnel augment the selling effort of order getters by performing a variety of services."

Three common types of sales support personnel are:

> Missionary salespeople
> Sales engineer
> Team selling

Match the correct type of sales support personnel to the example below:

1. _____ Ms. Wachter specializes in preparing promotions and information packets to hospitals and physicians. Her services help promote the purchase of new pharmaceutical products even though she is not directly involved in soliciting orders.

2. _____ A major computer firm routinely sends out three people when making sales calls; one person explains the technical capabilities of the equipment, one person explains the software capabilities and how the software fits the company's needs, and the third is responsible for arranging logistics such as price, delivery, and installation.

3. _____ Mr. Friedman is an expert in electrical engineering; however, he works in the sales department. He does not solicit sales but instead provides any and all information concerning the electrical function of the product his company manufactures and sells.

THE PERSONAL SELLING PROCESS

"The personal selling process consists of six stages:"

> Prospecting
> Preapproach
> Approach
> Presentation
> Close
> Follow-up

Match the correct stage of the selling process to the examples or statements listed below:

1. _____ Use the trial or assumptive approach to obtain a commitment of sale.

2. _____ Create a desire for the product by paying special attention to the customer's needs. Incorporate any of several methods to highlight the product, allay fears, and provide information.

3. _____ Gather information through personal observation, sales staff, and/or other customers, to find the best way to introduce yourself and your product to a new customer.

4. _____ Resolve any unsolved problems, ensure customer satisfaction.

5. _____ Use advertising, referrals, cold canvassing, etc. to search for and qualify potential customers.

6. _____ Make a good first impression. Gain the prospect's interest through reference to common acquaintances, a referral, or product demonstration.

PROSPECTING

"Personal selling begins with prospecting, the search for and qualification of potential customers."

There are three types of prospects:

    Lead
    Prospect
    Qualified buyer

I. Match the type of prospect to the definition below:

1. _____ A customer who wants and needs a product.

2. _____ The name of a person who may be a possible customer.

3. _____ A person who wants a product, can afford the product, and has the decision power to buy the product.

*Challenge - There are numerous ways of generating leads or prospects including advertising, coupons, toll-free numbers, exhibition fairs, and cold canvassing. If you sold the following items, which method of lead generation would you choose, and why? (You may choose methods not listed.)

1. Woks   3. Solar panels
2. Surgical instruments   4. Automobiles

II. There is a definite distinction made between the approach and preapproach stages.

Think of two contrasting sales encounters you have experienced in your own life. Choose one that was effective and one that was ineffective. List several reasons for the success or failure and relate them to the approach or preapproach stages of the personal selling process.

PRESENTATION

"The presentation is at the core of the selling process, and its objective is to convert a prospect into a consumer by creating a desire for the product or service."

There are three types of presentation format:

> Stimulus-response format
> Formula-selling format
> Need-satisfaction format

Match the type of selling presentation with the examples or statements below:

1. _____ A popular version of this format is the "canned" sales presentation.

2. _____ After you select a new Gant dress shirt, the salesperson suggests a matching club tie.

3. _____ This format emphasizes probing and listening by the salesperson to identify needs and interests of prospective buyers.

4. _____ The salesperson tries many appeals, hoping to "hit the right button."

5. _____ This approach is most consistent with the marketing concept.

6. _____ This format is commonly used in telephone and door-to-door selling and treats every prospect the same regardless of differences in needs or preferences.

OBJECTIONS

"Whether valid or not, experienced salespeople know that objections do not put an end to the presentation."

There are six common methods of responding to objections:

Ignore the objection
Acknowledge and convert the objection
Postpone the objection
Agree and neutralize
Accept the objection
Denial

Match the correct response to objections to the statements below.

1._____A technique by which the salesperson lets the prospect express such views, probe for the reason behind it, and attempt to stimulate discussion on the objections.

2._____This technique is used when it appears that the objection is a stalling mechanism or is clearly not important to the prospect.

3._____This technique is used when the objection will be dealt with later in the presentation.

4._____This technique is used when a prospect's objection is clearly untrue and based on misinformation.

5._____This technique involves using the objection as a reason for buying.

6._____A technique by which the salesperson agrees with the objection then shows that it is unimportant.

CLOSE

"The closing stage in the selling process involves obtaining a purchase commitment from the prospect."

There are three common closing methods:

> Trial close
> Assumptive close
> Urgency close

Match the correct type of close to the statements below:

1. _____This technique involves asking the prospect to make a decision on some aspect of the purchase.

2. _____This technique is used to commit the prospect quickly by making reference to the timeliness of the purchase.

3. _____This technique entails asking the prospect to make choices concerning delivery, warranty, or financing terms.

FOLLOW-UP

"The selling process does not end with the closing of a sale."

List four reasons why follow-up is such an important policy.

1. _____

2. _____

3. _____

4. _____

SETTING SALES FORCE OBJECTIVES

"Objectives are set for the total sales force and for each salesperson."

There are three common sales force objectives:

Output related -   dollar sales, unit sales volume, number of
                          new customers, etc.

Input related -   number of sales contacts, number of sales
                          calls, selling expenses, etc.

Behaviourally related -   product knowledge, customer service,
                          communication skills, etc.

Write two sales objectives for each of the three types of sales
objectives.

Output -   1. _____

             2. _____

Input -   1. _____

             2. _____

Behaviour - 1. _____

             2. _____

Note: Remember that any objective or set of objectives should be: (1) easy
to understand, (2) quantified as to the exact goal and specific time period
involved, (3) realistic, i.e., attainable, (4) compatible with other company
goals/objectives, and (5) hierarchically related.

ORGANIZING THE SALES FORCE

There are three special considerations when establishing a sales organization:

1. Should the company use its own sales force or should it use independent agents as manufacturer's representatives?

2. Should company salespeople be organized by geography, customer type, or product or service?

3. How many salespeople should be employed?

I. Which of the following statements describes a <u>company sales force</u>, and which statements describe <u>independent agents</u>?

1. _____Sales effort is enhanced because salespeople represent one firm, not several.

2. _____There is little fixed cost, mostly variable costs so the firm isn't burdened with overhead.

3. _____There is no cost to the firm to select, train, or supervise salespeople.

4. _____Company can transfer salespeople and change customer selling practices.

*Challenge - Use the formula in the text to figure at what point it is more financially sound to use independent agents, given:

    fixed cost = $350,000
    company sales commission = 2.5%
    independent agent commission = 6%

"If a company elects to employ its own salespeople, then it must choose an organizational structure based on (1) geography, (2) customer, or (3) product/service.

II. Which type of organizational structure is best described by the statements below:

1. _____This structure minimizes travel time, expenses, and duplication of selling effort.

2. _____When specialized knowledge is required to sell certain types of products, this structure is suggested.

3. _____When different buyers have different needs, this structure is suggested.

4. _____This structure often leads to higher administrative costs since two or more separate sales forces represent the same products.

5. _____Reporting to the General Sales Manager are the Eastern and Western Regional Sales Managers.

6. _____At Magic Micros, John sells the company's line of six microcomputers to existing customers and prospects in his territory. About once a week John will meet his friend Jane (who also works for Magic) in a customer's waiting room. Jane sells the company's line of specialized software and consulting services.

"The third question related to sales force organization involves determining the optimum size for the sales force."

$$NS = (NC \times CF \times CL) / AST$$
NS = Number of salespeople
NC = Number of customers
CF = Call frequency
CL = Average call length
AST = Average selling time available per sales person per year

III. Apple Computer has 15,000 retail outlets and company policy mandates at least one call per month per store. An average sales call takes 3 hours. Each Apple salesperson spends 50% of each 2000-hour work year selling. Use the workload method to determine the number of salespeople Apple needs to service these accounts.

$$NS = \text{_____}$$

SALES PLAN IMPLEMENTATION

The three main steps in implementing a sales plan are:

1. Sales force recruitment and selection
2. Sales force training
3. Sales force motivation and compensation

I. Write a sample job analysis for one of the following positions:

1. Computer salesperson
2. Piano salesperson
3. Marketing textbook salesperson

*Challenge - Attempt to find out about the training programs for three companies you would consider working for if you were in sales. Ask about such things as length of training, type of training, where the training is performed, and how you would be compensated during training.

"Salespeople are paid by using one of three plans:"

Straight salary compensation plan
Straight commission compensation plan
Combination compensation plan

II. Each method has special uses, advantages, and disadvantages. Which methods of compensation are being described by the examples or statements below:

1. _____ Provides little incentive, necessitates close supervision of salespersons.

2. _____ Especially useful when highly aggressive selling is required.

3. _____ Provides salesperson with maximum amount of security.

4. _____ Provides a certain amount of financial security while still providing some financial incentive.

5. _____ Selling expenses less predictable, may be difficult to administer.

6. _____ Offers the least financial security.

7. _____ Provides maximum amount of incentive.

8. _____ Especially useful when sales territories have relatively similar sales potentials.

9. _____ Especially useful when compensating new salespeople.

10. _____ "The sales training program is one year long. We'll pay you $18,000 during that time."

11. _____ "After your training program you will be paid $10,000 plus 3% of total dollar sales, plus you are eligible for a year-end bonus determined by your district's performance relative to all other districts.

12. _____ "After your training program you will be paid 4% on total dollar volume up to $10 million. Any sales in excess of $10 million commands a rate of 6%."

QUICK RECALL

I. What are the three major types of personal selling?

1. _____

2. _____

3. _____

II. What are the three types of sales support personnel?

1. _____

2. _____

3. _____

III. What are the six stages in the personal selling process?

1. _____

2. _____

3. _____

4. _____

5. _____

6. _____

IV. What are the three types of prospects?

1. _____

2. _____

3. _____

V. What are the three types of presentation formats?

1. _____

2. _____

3. _____

VI. What are the six ways of handling objections?

1. _____

2. _____

3. _____

4. _____

5. _____

6. _____

VII. What are the three common closing methods?

1. _____

2. _____

3. _____

VIII. What are four reasons why follow-up is an important policy?

1. _____

2. _____

3. _____

4. _____

IX. What are three common salesforce objectives?

1. _____

2. _____

3. _____

X. What are the three main steps in implementing a sales plan?

1. _____

2. _____

3. _____

XI. What are the three types of compensation plans?

1. _____

2. _____

3. _____

TERMS AND DEFINITIONS

1. team selling
2. sales plan
3. straight salary compensation plan
4. order-getter
5. personal selling process
6. account management policies
7. job analysis
8. order-taker
9. need-satisfaction presentation
10. workload method
11. sales engineer
12. stimulus-response presentation
13. sales management
14. straight commission compensation plan
15. personal selling
16. formula-selling presentation
17. combination compensation plan
18. missionary salespeople

COMPARING ORDER-TAKERS AND ORDER-GETTERS

1. order-taker
2. order-getter
3. order-getter
4. order-taker
5. order-taker
6. order-getter
7. order-taker
8. order-taker
9. order-taker
10. order-getter
11. order-getter
12. order-getter

SALES SUPPORT PERSONNEL

1. missionary salespeople
2. team selling
3. sales engineer

THE PERSONAL SELLING PROCESS

1. close
2. presentation
3. preapproach
4. follow-up
5. prospecting
6. approach

PROSPECTING

I.
1. prospect
2. lead
3. qualified buyer

II. There are many possible correct answers. For further guidance refer to your text page(s): 501-502.

PRESENTATION

1. formula-selling format
2. stimulus-response format
3. need-satisfaction format
4. stimulus-response format
5. need-satisfaction format
6. formula-selling format

OBJECTIONS

1. accept the objection
2. ignore the objection
3. postpone the objection

4. denial
5. acknowledge and convert the objection
6. agree and neutralize

CLOSE

1. trial close
2. urgency close
3. assumptive close

FOLLOW-UP

1. good customer relations
2. free publicity or references
3. feedback for new product changes
4. return customers

There are many possible correct answers. For further guidance refer to your text page(s): 506.

SETTING SALES FORCE OBJECTIVES

There are many possible correct answers. For further guidance refer to your text page(s): 507.

ORGANIZING THE SALES FORCE

I. 1. company sales force
    2. agents
    3. agents
    4. company sales force

II. 1. geography
    2. product
    3. customer
    4. customer
    5. geography
    6. product

III. NS = (15,000 x 12 x 3) / (2,000 x .50) = 540 salespeople

SALES PLAN IMPLEMENTATION

I. There are many possible correct answers. For further guidance refer to your text page(s): 511. Be sure your writing is neat, thorough, but concise.

II. 1. straight salary compensation plan
   2. straight commission compensation plan
   3. straight salary compensation plan
   4. combination compensation plan
   5. combination compensation plan
   6. straight commission compensation plan
   7. straight commission compensation plan
   8. combination compensation plan
   9. straight salary compensation plan
   10. straight salary compensation plan
   11. combination compensation plan
   12. straight commission compensation plan

QUICK RECALL

I. 1. order-taker
   2. order-getter
   3. sales-support personnel
II. 1. missionary
   2. sales engineer
   3. team selling

III. 1. prospecting
   2. preapproach
   3. approach
   4. presentation
   5. close
   6. follow-up

IV. 1. lead
   2. prospect
   3. qualified buyer

V. 1. stimulus-response format
   2. formula selling format
   3. needs satisfaction format

VI. 1. accept the objection
   2. ignore the objection
   3. postpone the objection
   4. denial
   5. acknowledge and convert the objection
   6. agree and neutralize

VII. 1. trial
   2. urgency close
   3. assumptive close

VIII. 1. good customer relations
   2. free publicity or references
   3. feedback for new product changes
   4. return customers

IX. 1. output related
   2. input related
   3. behaviourally related

X. 1. salesforce recruitment and selection
       2. salesforce training
       3. salesforce motivation and compensation

XI. 1. straight salary compensation plan
        2. straight commission compensation plan
        3. combination compensation plan

19

THE STRATEGIC MARKETING PROCESS

TERMS AND DEFINITIONS

Listed below are the definitions of important strategic marketing terms. Choose the correct term for each definition from the list below, and write it in the space provided.

Action item list
Annual marketing plans
Contribution margin analysis
Expense-to-sales ratio
Functional groupings
Generic marketing strategy
Geographical groupings
Goals
Industry
Line positions
Long range plans
Marketing audit

Marketing program
Marketing strategies
Product (program) champion
Product line groupings
Profitability analysis
Sales analysis
Sales component analysis
Sales response function
Staff positions
Strategic marketing process
Sustainable competitive
  advantage

1. _____A plan which deals with the marketing goals and strategies for a product, product line, or entire firm
for a single year.

2. _____A group of firms producing products which are close
substitutes for each other.

3. _____The relationship between the dollars of marketing
effort expended the marketing results of interest,
such as sales revenue, profit, or units sold.

4. _____A strategy which can be adopted by any firm,
regardless of the product or industry involved, to
achieve a sustainable competitive advantage.

5. _____Continuing efforts by an organization to allocate
its marketing mix resources to reach its target
market; involves phases of planning, implementation,
and control.

6. _____A written document approved by higher management
that a marketing manager uses to record and
communicate the result of planning (the goals and
marketing strategies) so marketing personnel can
implement it.

7. _____ A firm's strength relative to competitors' strengths in the markets they serve and the products they offer.

8. _____ Precise statements of results sought, quantified in terms of time and magnitude, where possible.

9. _____ A plan which deals with the marketing goals and strategies for a product, product line, or entire firm and covers from two to five years.

10. _____ Actions characterized by a specified target and a marketing program to reach it. The means by which goals are to be achieved.

11. _____ Tracing sales revenues back to their sources such as specific products, sales territories, or customers.

12. _____ People in these positions have the authority and responsibility to issue orders to people who report to them.

13. _____ Measuring the profitability of the firm's products, customer groups, sales territories and regions, channels of distribution, and order sizes.

14. _____ An aid to implementing a marketing plan which consists of three columns: (1) the task, (2) the name of the person responsible for completing the task, and (3) the date by which the task is to be finished.

15. _____ A form of profitability analysis which spotlights the behavior of controllable costs and indicates the contribution to profit of a specific marketing factor.

16. _____ Organizational divisions based on areas such as marketing, finance, R & D, etc.

17. _____ A comprehensive, unbiased, periodic review of a firm's, or an SBU's strategic marketing process.

18. _____ People in an organization who have the responsibility to advise people in line positions but cannot issue direct orders to them.

19. _____ A unit subdivided according to offerings for which it is responsible.

20. _____ A form of ratio analysis in which specific costs or expenses are expressed as a percentage of sales revenue.

21. _____ Organizational divisions based on geographical location.

22._____A tool used for controlling marketing programs in which actual sales records are compared with sales goals to identify strengths and weaknesses.

23._____An individual within a firm whose job it is to cut red tape and move a product or program forward.

SUSTAINABLE COMPETITIVE ADVANTAGE

"Marketing executives search continuously to find a competitive advantage - a strength relative to their competitors in some market niche - in the market they serve and the products they offer . . . ."

List ten types of competitive advantages one firm may have over another. Try to name a company that enjoys each advantage.

For example: breadth of product line, IBM.

1. _____

2. _____

3. _____

4. _____

5. _____

6. _____

7. _____

8. _____

9. _____

10. _____

SITUATION ANALYSIS

"The first element of the planning phase of the strategic marketing process is situation analysis."

Check which information is needed for a <u>thorough</u> situation analysis.

1. _____Information about your company's past and current revenues, expenses, profits, and growth rate by segment and in total.

2. _____Information about your competitors' past and current revenues, expenses, profits, and growth rates by segment and in total (if possible).

3. _____Information about the industry's past and current profits, revenues, expenses, and growth rate.

4. _____Projected totals of profits, revenues, expenses, and growth rates for your company, your competitors, and the industry.

GOAL SETTING

There are two essential elements to goal setting. They are:

   1.   Goals should be quantified in terms of how much and timing.
   2.   Senior management must be involved.

List at least two reasons why each of the elements listed above are essential for effective goal setting.

1. _____

2. _____

3. _____

4. _____

THE MARKETING PROGRAM

"A generic marketing strategy is one that can be adopted by any firm, regardless of the product or industry involved."

If a business firm wants to increase profits, it can attempt to:

   1. Increase revenues
   2. Decrease expenses
   3. Do both (increase revenues and decrease expenses)

I. List four possible ways of increasing revenues.

    1. _____

    2. _____

    3. _____

    4. _____

II. List three possible ways of decreasing expenses.

    1. _____

    2. _____

    3. _____

FRAMEWORKS TO IMPROVE MARKETING PLANNING

"Marketing planning is a complex task. However, there are two techniques that are helpful for making important strategy and resource allocation decisions:

Sales Response Function
Market-product grid

I   SALES RESPONSE FUNCTIONS

". . . Having identified this competitive advantage, they must allocate their firm's resources to exploit it."

In theory, companies use the sales response function to relate the expense of marketing effort to the marketing results obtained. They also use the concept of maximizing incremental revenue minus incremental cost.

Answer the following questions concerning the theoretical aspects of effective resource allocation:

1. In what ways does this concept parallel marginal revenue/marginal cost analysis (Chapter 11)?

_____

_____

_____

2. When a sales response function is plotted on a graph, what do we list on the horizontal axis?

_____

_____

_____

3. What is the explanation for the S-shape of a sales response function?

_____

_____

_____

4. Given the following information, what is the ratio of incremental sales revenue to incremental effort?

Increase in marketing effort went from two million to four million. Increase in sales revenue went from 33 million to 57 million.

Answer: _____

II.   **MARKET-PRODUCT GRID**

"A market-product grid acts as a framework for relating market segments to products offered or potential marketing actions by a firm. This type of evaluation suggests several alternative strategies."

Market-product concentration
Market specialization
Product specialization
Selective specialization
Full coverage

A. Match the above strategies to the appropriate diagram below:

1. _____

2. _____

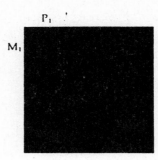

3. _____

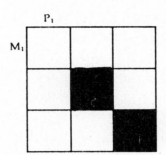

4. _____

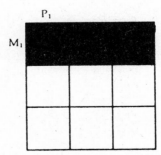

5. _____

"The market-product grid also clarifies trade-offs available in the diversification matrix (described in Chapter 2)

B. Answer the following questions using the market-product grid below:

	Hot	Sweetened Cold	Unsweetened Cold
0-5 years	1	2	3
6-18 years	4	5	6
19+ years	7	8	9

1. _____ Which cells would be darkened if the strategy is to specialize in cereals for children from infant to five years old?

2. _____ Suppose there are three competitors in the industry. Competitor A's strategy is to specialize in the 19 or over age group. Competitor B markets a broad line of cold sweetened cereals with separate products targeted to each age group. Competitor C specializes in infant hot cereals. In which cells might there be opportunities for new entries?

3. _____ Which cells would be darkened if you wanted to develop product specialization in cold unsweetened cereals?

STRENGTHS AND WEAKNESSES OF MARKET-PRODUCT GRIDS

List three strengths and two weaknesses in using market-product grids.

Strengths:

1. _____

2. _____

3. _____

Weaknesses:

1. _____

2. _____

REQUIREMENTS OF AN EFFECTIVE MARKETING PLAN

"Plans are nothing; planning is everything."
                              -Dwight D. Eisenhower-

List the five basic elements for effective market planning and plans:

1. _____

2. _____

3. _____

4. _____

5. _____

PROBLEMS IN MARKETING, PLANNING, AND STRATEGY

"The best laid plans of mice and men sometimes go awry."
                              -William Shakespeare-

List five major areas where problems can occur in the planning phase of a firm's strategic marketing process:

1. _____

2. _____

3. _____

4. _____

5. _____

IMPROVING IMPLEMENTATION OF MARKETING PROGRAMS

"No magic formula exists to guarantee effective implementation of marketing plans. In fact, the answer seems to be equal parts of good management, attention to detail, and plain common sense."

However, some guidelines can be identified:

1. Communicate goals and the means to achieve them.
2. Have a responsible program "champion" willing to act.
3. Have doers benefit personally from successful program implementation.
4. Take action and avoid "paralysis by analysis."
5. Foster open communications to force problems to the surface.
6. Schedule precise tasks, responsibilities, and deadlines.

I   Using specific information from the text, find company examples that best exemplify these six guidelines.

1. _____

2. _____

3. _____

4. _____

5. _____

6. _____

ROLE OF THE PRODUCT MANAGER

"The function of a product manager is to plan, implement, and control the annual and long-range plans for the product(s) for which she is responsible."

I.   List six primary tasks of the Product Manager/Brand Manager/Marketing Manager.

1. _____

2. _____

3. _____

4. _____

5. _____

6. _____

"There are both benefits and dangers to the product manager system used by many consumer and industrial products companies."

II. List both the advantages and disadvantages of the product manager system.

Advantages	Disadvantages
1. _____	1. _____
2. _____	2. _____
3. _____	3. _____
4. _____	4. _____

I.   What activities are involved when a marketing manager uses management-by-exception to identify deviations?

1. _____

2. _____

3. _____

SALES ANALYSIS

There are three methods used to control marketing programs:

> Sales analysis
> Profitability analysis
> Marketing audits

I.   List six possible types of various breakdowns used in sales analysis and explain why they would be useful.

1. _____
   _____

2. _____
   _____

3. _____
   _____

4. _____
   _____

5. _____
   _____

6. _____
   _____

*Challenge - Think of other useful information breakdowns and explain why or how they would be useful.

NOTE: Question II is only for students who have access to a microcomputer. If you do not have access, please do exercise III instead. (Of course, it wouldn't hurt to do both!)

II. Contribution margin analysis, a form of profitability analysis, spotlights the behavior of controllable costs and indicates the contribution to profit for specific marketing factors. Turn to Figure 20-8 in your text. Use a microcomputer and a spreadsheet program such as Lotus 1-2-3 or Multiplan to develop a spreadsheet which will perform all the calculations in Figure 20-8. (Use the data given in the figure. After you do this, perform several "sensitivity analyses" to see what happens . . . if Taylor's selling costs increase by 2 percent, etc. Try several "what if" analyses. It's as easy as 1-2-3!

III. Expense-to-sales ratio

In Figure 19-8 the numbers indicate that salesman Taylor has higher sales revenue and lower costs (as a percent of sales). Can you think of any factors that could influence the figures in such a way that Taylor was really only equal to his peers in productivity, rather than superior?

QUICK RECALL

I. What are the three phases in the strategic marketing process?

1. _____

2. _____

3. _____

II. List the three steps in the planning phase of the strategic marketing process.

1. _____

2. _____

3. _____

III. List the four generic marketing strategies to increase revenue.

1. _____

2. _____

3. _____

4. _____

IV. What are two techniques that are helpful for making important strategy and resource allocation decisions?

1. _____

2. _____

V. What are five alternative marketing strategies suggested by market-product grids?

1. _____

2. _____

3. _____

4. _____

5. _____

VI   There are three methods used to control marketing programs.

1. _____

2. _____

3. _____

TERMS AND DEFINITIONS

1. annual marketing plan
2. industry
3. sales response function
4. generic marketing strategy
5. strategic marketing process
6. marketing program
7. competitive advantage
8. goals (or objectives)
9. long-range plans
10. marketing strategies
11. sales component analysis
12. line positions
13. profitability analysis
14. action item list
15. contribution margin analysis
16. functional groupings
17. marketing audit
18. staff positions
19. product line groupings
20. expense-to-sales ratio
21. geographic groupings
22. sales analysis
23. product or program champion

SUSTAINABLE COMPETITIVE ADVANTAGE

There are many possible correct answers. For further guidance refer to your text pages(s): 520

SITUATION ANALYSIS

1. yes
2. yes
3. yes
4. yes

ALL OF THESE AREAS ARE ESSENTIAL!

GOAL SETTING

1. A quantified goal provides a performance standard
2. A quantified goal is apt to be more easily communicated and understood
3. Involvement by senior management provides a check on the realism and consistency of goals.
4. Involvement by senior management integrates more managerial experience into the planning process.

THE MARKETING PROGRAM

I. 1. market penetration
    2. product development
    3. market development
    4. diversification

II. 1. experience curve effects
    2. economies of scale
    3. cost-cutting measures

FRAMEWORKS TO IMPROVE MARKET PLANNING

I   SALES RESPONSE FUNCTION

1. An action is favorable as long as incremental return exceeds incremental cost.
2. marketing expenditures
3. The curve is S-shaped because of the diminishing marginal returns of additional marketing expenditures.
4. (57-33)/(4-2)= 12:1

II.   MARKET PRODUCT GRID

A.   1. product specialization
     2. full coverage
     3. selective specialization
     4. market specialization
     5. market-product concentration

B.   1. cells 1,2,3
     2. cells 3,4,6
     3. cells 3,6,9

STRENGTHS AND WEAKNESSES OF MARKET-PRODUCT GRIDS

STRENGTHS:

1. Helps identify potential opportunities to fill market niches or product gaps for the firm.

2. Highlights potential economies of scale in marketing, R & D, or manufacturing that result from entering new markets or offering new products.

3. Shows potential revenue losses caused by product cannibalism.

WEAKNESSES:

1. Have to form meaningful market segments.
2. Have to form useful product clusters.

REQUIREMENTS OF AN EFFECTIVE MARKETING PLAN

1. measurable, achievable objectives
2. a base of valid assumptions
3. simple, clear, and specific plans
4. complete and feasible plans
5. controllable and flexible plans

PROBLEMS IN MARKETING, PLANNING, AND STRATEGY

1. Formula Planning frameworks may assume that past trends will continue into future. Formula Planning may provide a tip-off to competition.
2. Plans based on poor assumptions about changing environments.
3. Planners lost sight of their customers.
4. Too much time and effort spent in data collection and analysis.
5. Planning had drifted away from being the responsibility of line managers into the hands of the "professional planners."

IMPROVING IMPLEMENTATION OF MARKETING PROGRAMS

There are many possible correct answers. For further guidance refer to your text page(s): 537-540.

Make sure you have answered these questions or prepared these exercises as if you were up for promotion.

ROLE OF THE PRODUCT MANAGER

I. 1. Preparing annual marketing plans, sales forecasts, and budgets
    2. Developing long-range competitive strategies
    3. Developing sales force and distributor support for the product
    4. Working with advertising agencies
    5. Gathering marketing research
    6. Improving existing products and creating new ones

II. Advantages

    1. strong advocate system
    2. flexible system
    3. profit & loss responsibility pinpointed
    4. balance of marketing/non-marketing activities

Disadvantages

    1. little or no direct authority
    2. support gained through persuasion
    3. can develop little functional expertise
    4. short-term reward orientation

THE MARKETING CONTROL PROCESS

I. 1. measuring quantitative results
    2. measuring qualitative results
    3. taking marketing actions

SALES ANALYSIS

I. 1. customer characteristics/demographics
    2. product characteristics
    3. order size
    4. price or discount class
    5. commission to the sales representative
    6. geographic characteristics

II. This exercise is only designed for students who have access to a micro computer. If you do not have access, please just do exercise III.

III. To answer this question, you need to analyze salesperson Taylor's sales for each product and consider his sales versus territorial potential. Taylor could be concentrating selling efforts only on high-margin products. Taylor's territory could have extraordinarily high potential, thus making sales easier.

QUICK RECALL

I.   1. planning
     2. implementation
     3. control

II. 1. situation analysis
     2. goal setting
     3. marketing program

III. 1. market penetration
     2. product development
     3. market development
     4. diversification

IV. 1. sales response function
     2. market-product grid

V.   1. market specialization
     2. product specialization
     3. selective specialization
     4. full coverage
     5. market-product concentration

VI   1. sales analysis
     2. profitability analysis
     3. marketing

20

INTERNATIONAL MARKETING

TERMS AND DEFINITIONS

Listed below are the definitions of important international marketing terms. Choose the correct term for each definition from the list below, and write it in the space provided.

Balance of trade
Blocked currency
Boycotts
Contract manufacturing
Counter trade
Culture
Customized approach
Customs
Direct exporting
Direct investment
Dumping
Duties
Economic infrastructure

Exporting
Expropriation
Foreign assembly
Global approach
Indirect exporting
International marketing
Joint venture
Licensing
Quotas
Tariffs
Transnational corporation
Values

1. _____Marketing across international boundaries.

2. _____Having another firm sell products in a foreign country.

3. _____A method that entails designing a different marketing plan for each nation recognizing the different needs, values, customs, languages, and purchasing power of each nation.

4. _____Currency which a government will not allow to be converted into other currencies.

5. _____An investment in an assembly or manufacturing plant located in a foreign country.

6. _____When a company or its assets taken over by the host country.

7. _____Using foreign labour to assemble parts and components which have been shipped to that country.

8. _____Marketing through an intermediary involves the least amount of commitment and risk, but will probably return the least profit.

9. _____ A marketing approach that assumes that product use and the needs it satisfies are universal, and need not be adjusted for each country.

10. _____ The act of selling products internationally below their domestic prices.

11. _____ Special taxes on imports.

12. _____ A nation's communication, transportation, financial, and distribution networks.

13. _____ The norms and expectations about the way people do things in a particular country.

14. _____ A refusal to deal with a country - usually to express disapproval or enforce certain conditions.

15. _____ When a company handles its own exports, without the use of intermediaries.

16. _____ A company that has a global orientation to marketing its products.

17. _____ The religious or moral beliefs of a country or its people.

18. _____ When a company offers the right to a trademark, patent, trade secret, or other valued items of intellectual property in return for a royalty or fee.

19. _____ A schedule or series of duties imposed by a government on imported or exported goods.

20. _____ Agreeing to have another firm manufacture products according to certain specifications. If the manufacturing firm is a foreign one, the products may then be sold in the foreign country or exported back to the home country.

21. _____ Legal limits placed on the amount and/or number of products allowed to enter a country.

22. _____ The sense of values, ideas, and attitudes of a homogeneous group of people that are transmitted from one generation to the next.

23. _____ Using barter rather than money in making international sales.

24. _____ When a foreign country and a local concern invest together to create a local business.

25. _____ The difference between the monetary value of a nation's exports and imports.

WHY FIRMS UNDERTAKE INTERNATIONAL MARKETING

"International marketing of goods and services as a major part of the Canadian Economy."

I. List six major reasons Canadian firms go international:

1. _____

2. _____

3. _____

4. _____

5. _____

6. _____

II. List seven foreign-owned corporations in Canada.

1. _____

2. _____

3. _____

4. _____

5. _____

6. _____

7. _____

GLOBAL VS. CUSTOMIZED PRODUCT STRATEGY

"As international marketing grows; firms selling both consumer and industrial products in foreign countries face a dilemma: should they use a global or customized strategy for the products they sell."

Globalized approach
Customized approach

Which of the following examples demonstrate a company using a global approach and which are using a customized approach?

1. _____McDonald's serves carbonated beverages in Kansas, beer in Germany, and sake in Japan.

2. _____Eastman Kodak includes language keys tailored to individual countries on the copier control panel, and provides reduction capability for different page sizes.

3. _____ A fast food franchise keeps the same uniforms for all its employees; short skirts, and halter tops.

4. _____ When Xerox first introduced its copiers into Great Britain, they failed to accommodate for differences in the width of the doorways.

ASSESSING ENVIRONMENTAL FACTORS

There are three essential environmental factors to consider when contemplating the international market:

> Economic conditions
> Political and legal conditions
> Cultural factors

I. Economic Conditions

There are three main classifications of countries in terms of economic growth:

> Developed
> Developing
> Communist

A.   Decide whether the following examples or statements describe a developed, developing, or communist classification of economic growth.

1. _____ These countries are in the process of moving from an agricultural to industrial economy.

2. _____ These countries, which include the USSR and Cuba, have significant legal and political barriers when dealing economically with the United States. These markets are just beginning to be tapped, especially since Gorbachev's "perestroika" policy.

3. _____ These countries still remain locked in pre-industrial economies, living standards are low, and show little promise of improvement.

4. _____ Private enterprise dominates, although they have substantial public sectors as well.

II. Political and Legal Conditions

Three important factors affect political and legal conditions:

Government attitude
Stability
Bureaucracy

Using the most recent issues of newspapers, magazines, journals, etc., find true life examples of how each of the factors (government attitude, stability, and bureaucracy) have affected Canadian companies operating abroad.

III. Cultural Factors

How would the following factors (language, customs, and values) affect international marketing strategies. Choose two and discuss them thoroughly.

1. In France men wear more cosmetics than women do.

2. In India the cow is considered sacred.

3. Business people in South America prefer to negotiate in very close physical proximity.

4. Salad dressing that doesn't come in a tube won't be popular in Germany.

5. In Japanese, "sticks like crazy" means it sticks foolishly.

6. In Italy it is improper for a man to call on a woman if she is home alone.

IV STABILITY AND FINANCIAL POLICIES

There are many potential hazards that are built into international marketing:

> Threats of physical violence against personnel
> Duties
> Blocked currency
> Tariffs
> Boycotts
> Expropriation

Use periodicals (newspapers, magazines, journals) to find current examples of each of the potential difficulties listed above.

EVALUATING ALTERNATIVES FOR INTERNATIONAL OPERATIONS

I. There are five basic modes of entry into international marketing:

> Joint ventures
> Direct exporting
> Direct investment
> Licensing
> Indirect exporting

Each method of entry provides a different potential level of profitability and risk. List the forms of entry from least amount of risk to greatest amount of risk and explain why.

1. _____

_____

_____

_____

2. _____

_____

_____

_____

3. _____

_____

_____

_____

4. _____

_____

_____

_____

5. _____

_____

_____

_____

II. Exporting

There are two main types of exporting:

Indirect exporting
Direct exporting

List two examples of companies or corporations that deal exclusively with indirect or direct exporting.

III. Licensing

"Under licensing, a company offers the right to a trademark, patent, trade secret, or other valued item in return for a royalty or fee."

A. List the advantages and disadvantages of licensing.

Advantages	Disadvantages
1. _____	1. _____
_____	_____
2. _____	2. _____
_____	_____
	3. _____
	_____

B. There are two forms of licensing:

Contract manufacturing
Foreign assembly

Though both forms of licensing are used successfully, they can be criticized on such grounds as inconsistent quality control, unfair labour practices, and/or peer ethics. Can you think of specific ways these criticisms may apply?

IV. Joint Ventures

"When a foreign company and a local concern invest together to create a local business, it is called a joint venture."

List both the advantages and disadvantages of a joint venture.

Advantages	Disadvantages
1. _____	1. _____
2. _____	2. _____

V. Direct Investment

"The biggest commitment a company can make when entering an international market is by direct investment, which entails actually investing in an assembly or manufacturing plant located in a foreign country."

List the five major advantages to direct investment.

1. _____

2. _____

3. _____

4. _____

5. _____

*Challenge - Although the above five statements reflect advantages, poor management can result in these advantages being turned into problems. What are these problems and how should they be avoided?

SELECTING A COUNTRY FOR ENTRY

Before a firm becomes involved in international marketing they should carefully consider five steps. Define or clarify the five steps listed below:

1. Specify marketing objectives.

_____

_____

_____

2. Choose single or multiple country strategy.

_____

_____

_____

3. Specify the candidate countries or regions to consider.

_____

_____

_____

4. Estimate the ROI for each of the candidates.

_____

_____

_____

5. Select one or more countries to enter.

_____

_____

_____

ESTABLISHING A MARKETING ORGANIZATION

"Once a country or group of countries has been selected for entry, an appropriate marketing organization must be established."

There are many types of organizational structures. List the four common types of organizational structures discussed in the text.

1. _____

2. _____

3. _____

4. _____

DESIGNING A MARKETING PROGRAM

"Because a foreign country is different from the Canada in many respects, careful marketing research is essential in developing a successful marketing program."

Information is needed from both primary and secondary sources.

I. List as many reliable secondary information sources as possible:

1. _____

2. _____

3. _____

4. _____

5. _____

II. Primary information may be more difficult to obtain in foreign countries than in Canada.

What strategies could you use to collect market research data given the following conditions:

1. You are marketing products for women in a country where women do not discuss worldly matters with men.

2. You need to collect large samples of information where questionnaires are not permitted through the mail.

THE MARKETING MIX

International marketers must understand how information received through market research will affect the marketing mix.

I. <u>Product</u> - The international marketer has three product options:

> Extension
> Adaptation
> Invention

Using the text and/or information from outside research, make a list of at least three examples of companies or products that demonstrate:

Product extension   1. _____

                          2. _____

                          3. _____

Product adaptation   1. _____

                          2. _____

                          3. _____

Product invention   1. _____

                          2. _____

                          3. _____

II. <u>Price</u> -

"Most companies use a cost-plus pricing strategy." Explain what effect this has on international firms.

_____

_____

_____

*Challenge - Many products are sold internationally below their domestic price. This practice is called dumping. Recently there has been a lot of controversy concerning the ethics of some firms selling items considered inferior or even harmful by Canadian standards. Have your instructor suggest a specific case for you to research. List the arguments of both sides.

III. <u>Promotion</u>   Many promotional mistakes have been made because of the failure to understand the cultural and logistical environment of a given country. Before you would begin promoting a tobacco product in Sweden, what types of questions should you ask? List as many as possible; refer to your text Chapter on promotion if necessary.

IV. <u>Place</u>   Another important variable is the channel between two nations, which moves the product from the domestic market to the foreign market.

There are three types of intermediaries that can handle this responsibility:

A resident buyer in the foreign country
An overseas representative for a foreign firm
An independent intermediary

Match the correct intermediary to the example or statements below:

1. _____ A wholesaler who works for foreign companies but resides in the exporter's country.

2. _____ A merchant or wholesaler who buys and sells the products, or an agent who brings buyers and sellers together.

3. _____ A person who works for foreign companies and resides in the destination country.

SEQUENCE OF DECISIONS IN ENTERING INTERNATIONAL MARKETING
(Figure 20-5)

Assess Environmental factors in International Markets	Evaluate Alternatives for International Operations	Tailor Marketing Program to the Country
-->	--->	

1._____   4._____   9._____

2._____   5._____   10._____

3._____   6._____   11._____

                  7._____

                  8._____

TERMS AND DEFINITIONS

1. international marketing
2. exporting
3. customized approach
4. blocked currency
5. direct investment
6. expropriation
7. foreign assembly
8. indirect exporting
9. global approach
10. dumping
11. duties
12. economic infrastructure
13. customs

14. boycott
15. direct exporting
16. transnational corporation
17. values
18. licensing
19. tariff
20. contract manufacturing
21. quotas
22. culture
23. counter trade
24. joint venture
25. balance of trade

WHY FIRMS UNDERTAKE INTERNATIONAL MARKETING

I.
1. To counter adverse demographic or economic factors in home market.
2. To reduce or avoid competition.
3. To extend a product's life cycle.
4. To enhance economies of scale in production and marketing.
5. To dispose of excess inventory.
6. To export and import new technology.

II. There are many possible correct answers. For further guidance refer to your text page(s): 564 (Figure 20-4).

GLOBAL VS. CUSTOMIZED PRODUCT STRATEGIES

1. customized
2. customized
3. global
4. global

ASSESSING ENVIRONMENTAL FACTORS

I. Economic Conditions

A.
1. developing
2. communist
3. developing
4. developed

B. Numerous possible correct answers. Be sure to list both type of currency and exchange rate.

II. Political and legal conditions

There are many possible correct answers. For further guidance refer to your text pages(s): 569-570.

III. Cultural Factors

There are many possible correct answers. For further guidance refer to your text pages(s): 570-572.

IV STABILITY AND FINANCIAL POLICIES

There are many possible correct answers. For further guidance refer to your text page(s): 570.

EVALUATING ALTERNATIVES FOR INTERNATIONAL OPERATIONS

I.
1. indirect exporting
2. direct exporting
3. licensing
4. joint ventures
5. direct investment

II. Exporting

There are many possible correct answers. For further guidance refer to your text page(s): 573.

III. Licensing

Advantages	Disadvantages
A. 1. low risk	1. loss of control
2. capital-free international market entry	2. don't share in profits
	3. reputation could be jeopardized

B. There are many possible correct answers. For further guidance refer to your text page(s): 573-574.

IV. Joint Ventures

Advantages	Disadvantages
1. synergy of combining resources	1. disagreements on goals/ priorities
2. can meet government requirements	2. differences in operating procedures

V. Direct Investment

1. cost economics
2. improved image
3. gain better marketing insight
4. greater control
5. fewer restrictions

SELECTING A COUNTRY FOR ENTRY

There are many possible correct answers. For further guidance refer to your text page(s): 575-576.

ESTABLISHING A MARKETING ORGANIZATION

1. export department
2. foreign subsidiary
3. international division
4. worldwide products division

DESIGNING A MARKETING PROGRAM

I.   1. Canadian Government Publications
      2. the United Nations
      3. the International Monetary Fund
      4. the host country's government
      5. host country publications

II.   There are many possible correct answers. For further guidance refer to
      your text page(s): 577-578.

MARKETING MIX

I, II, III: There are many possible correct answers. For further guidance
              refer to your text page(s):   577-582.

IV.   1. representative for foreign firms
      2. independent intermediary
      3. resident buyer in foreign country

QUICK RECALL

1.   Economic conditions
2.   Political & legal conditions
3.   Cultural factors
4.   Indirect exporting
5.   Direct exporting
6.   Licensing
7.   Joint ventures
8.   Direct investments
9.   Select the country/countries
10. Establish the marketing organization
11. Design and implement the marketing program.

21

MARKETING OF SERVICES

TERMS AND DEFINITIONS

Listed below are the definitions of important services marketing terms. Choose the correct term for each definition from the list below, and write it in the space provided.

Capacity management
Customer contact audit
Four I's of Services
Idle production capacity
Internal marketing

Off-peak pricing
Service continuum
Services

1. _____ A marketing philosophy based on the notion that a service organization must focus on its employees, or internal market, before successful programs can be directed at consumers.

2. _____ With regard to service, refers to a situation where the service provider is available, but there is no demand.

3. _____ Intangible benefits provided by an organization to consumers in exchange for money or some other value.

4. _____ A price setting approach in which the amount charged is a function of the variations of service demand changing with the time of day or day of week.

5. _____ Managing the demand for a service so that it is available to consumers.

6. _____ A flow chart of the points of interaction between a consumer and a service provider.

7. _____ The elements that make services unique in relation to products. They include intangibility, inconsistency, inseparability, and inventory.

8. _____ A range of products/services in terms of the degree of tangibility or intangibility involved.

THE FOUR I's OF SERVICES

"There are four unique elements to services . . ."

> Intangibility
> Inconsistency
> Inseparability
> Inventory

You have just graduated and are preparing to start your first full-time job in a city 1500 miles away. You have chosen a professional mover to transfer your belongings. Explain how each of the four I's applies to the moving company.

1. Intangibility_____

_____

2. Inconsistency_____

_____

3. Inseparability_____

_____

4. Inventory_____

_____

*Challenge - Find out if there is a peak season for moving, and if so, why is this?

THE SERVICE CONTINUUM

"As companies look at what they bring to the market there is a range from tangible to intangible, or product-dominant to service-dominant organizations referred to as the service continuum."

Arrange the following in rank-order from (1) most product-dominant to (13) most service-dominant entities.

_____Purina Puppy Chow

_____Levi's Jeans

_____Raisin Bran

_____On-Tour Travel

_____Junior College Professor

_____Licensed Practical Nurse

_____Sunflower Cablevision

_____Burger King

_____Theatre

_____Graphic's Advertising

_____Custom Bootmaker

_____Condominium

_____Toyota Dealer

CLASSIFYING SERVICES

Services can be classified in three different ways:

Delivered by people or equipment
Profit or nonprofit
Government-sponsored

Classify the services listed below into the most logical category:

1. _____Computer Dating Service

2. _____Health & Welfare Canada

3. _____MADD (Mothers Against Drunk Drivers)

4. _____Fantasy Massage

5. _____Revenue Canada

6. _____March of Dimes

7. _____Environment of Canada

8. _____General Contractors

9. _____Pest Control Service

HOW CONSUMERS PURCHASE SERVICES

I. There are three important factors to be considered during the purchase process:

> Search qualities
> Experience qualities
> Credence qualities

Match the correct quality to the statement or definition below.

1. _____Qualities which can only be discerned after purchase or during consumption.

2. _____These qualities are common to medical diagnoses and legal services.

3. _____Qualities which can be determined before purchase.

4. _____Services such as restaurants and child care have these qualities.

5. _____Qualities or characteristics which the consumer may find impossible to evaluate even after purchase and consumption.

6. _____Tangible goods such as jewelry, clothing, and furniture.

II. There are two basic dimensions which play an important part in purchase evaluation:

> Complexity -   The number and intricacy of the steps required for the service.
>
> Divergence -   The amount of latitude possible in the execution of the service.

Select three different types of restaurants in your area. Explain how they differ from one another in terms of complexity and divergence.

_____

_____

_____

_____

_____

_____

_____

III. "A customer contact audit is the flow chart of the points of interaction between a consumer and a service provider."

Trace the points of customer contact when using the drive-in window of a fast food restaurant.

_____

_____

_____

_____

_____

_____

_____

*Challenge - Explain how you, as a customer, could be dissatisfied (low range) or pleased (high point) at each customer contact point.

MARKETING MIX FOR SERVICES

Product

There are three areas of importance which should be considered in the product/service element of the marketing mix:

> Exclusivity
> Branding
> Capacity management

I.   Discuss whether you agree or disagree with the idea that services cannot be patented.

_____

_____

_____

_____

_____

II. What are possible branding strategies you could use if you owned a delivery service?

1. _____

2. _____

3. _____

4. _____

"Service organizations must manage the availability of their offerings to: (1) smooth demand over time so that demand matches capacity, and (2) ensure that the organization's assets are used in ways that will maximize the return on investment."

SETTING PRICES

"Pricing in services plays two roles: to affect consumer perceptions and to be used in capacity management."

I. Make a list of specific types of services in which a very low price might be a detriment to consumer perceptions.

1. _____

2. _____

3. _____

4. _____

5. _____

Make a list of specific types of services where a very high price would be a detriment to consumer perceptions.

6. _____

7. _____

8. _____

9. _____

10. _____

II. Make a list of at least five types of services which use off-peak pricing.

    1. _____

    2. _____

    3. _____

    4. _____

    5. _____

DISTRIBUTION

"Distribution is a major factor in developing a service marketing strategy because of the inseparability of services from the provider."

List four types of service businesses which have made changes in their distribution philosophy in order to be more competitive.

For example: <u>Banks - banking machines</u>

    1. _____

    2. _____

    3. _____

    4. _____

PROMOTION

"In service marketing, publicity can play a major role in promotional strategy."

Explain the advantages and disadvantages of using publicity.

Advantages:

1. _____

2._____

Disadvantages:

1._____

2._____

QUICK RECALL

I.   What are the four I's of services?

     1. _____

     2. _____

     3. _____

     4. _____

II. Name three ways of classifying services.

     1. _____

     2. _____

     3. _____

III. Name three areas of importance when considering the product/service
     element of the marketing mix.

     1. _____

     2. _____

     3. _____

ANSWERS

TERMS AND DEFINITIONS

1. internal marketing
2. idle production capacity
3. services
4. off-peak pricing
5. capacity management
6. customer contact audit
7. four I's of services
8. service continuum

THE FOUR I's OF SERVICES

There are many possible correct answers. For further guidance refer to your text page(s): 589-590.

THE SERVICE CONTINUUM

1. Raisin Bran
2. Levi's Jeans
3. Purina Puppy Chow
4. Condominium
5. Toyota Dealer
6. Custom Bootmaker
7. Burger King
8. Sunflower Cablevision
9. On-Tour Travel
10. Graphic's Advertising
11. Theatre
12. Licensed Practical Nurse
13. Junior College Professor

CLASSIFYING SERVICES

1. delivered
2. government-sponsored
3. profit or nonprofit
4. delivered
5. government-sponsored
6. profit or nonprofit
7. government-sponsored
8. delivered
9. delivered

HOW CONSUMERS PURCHASE SERVICES

I.
1. experience qualities
2. credence qualities
3. search qualities
4. experience qualities
5. credence qualities
6. search qualities

II.
There are many possible correct answers. For further guidance refer to your text page(s): 595.

III.
There are many possible correct answers. For further guidance refer to your text page(s): 595-596.

MARKETING MIX FOR SERVICES

I, II.   There are many possible correct answers. For further guidance refer
         to your text page(s): 598-599.

SETTING PRICES

I.   There are many possible correct answers. For further guidance refer to
      your text page(s):   600-601.

      1. physician   6. hotel
      2. lawyer   7. air travel
      3. management consultant   8. bus travel
      4. accountant   9. dry cleaning
      5. auto mechanic   10. amusement park

II.   1. telecommunications
      2. movies
      3. restaurants
      4. hospitals
      5. airlines

DISTRIBUTION

1.   fast food restaurants
2.   legal services
3.   tax preparation services
4.   health care outpatient clinics

PROMOTION

Advantages: 1. Publicity is free.
               2. Message delivered by a credible source.

Disadvantages: 1. No control over timing.
                  2. No control over who sees the message.

QUICK RECALL

I.   1. intangibility
      2. inconsistency
      3. inseparability
      4. inventory

II.   1. Whether they are delivered by people or equipment.
      2. Whether they are profit or nonprofit.
      3. Whether or not they are government sponsored.

III. 1. exclusivity
      2. branding
      3. capacity management